BREATHING
EACH OTHER'S AIR

Florence McNeil

POLESTAR
BOOK PUBLISHERS

Published by:
Polestar Press Ltd.
1011 Commercial Drive, Second Floor
Vancouver, BC
V5L 3X1

The Publisher would like to acknowledge the financial assistance of The Canada Council, British Columbia Cultural Services Branch, and the Department of Canadian Heritage.

Edited by Suzanne Bastedo.
Cover photograph by Dale Sanders, from the book **The Emerald Sea: Exploring the Underwater Wilderness of the North Pacific Coast** (Whitecap, 1993). Reprinted with permission.
Cover design by Jim Brennan.
Printed in Canada by Best-Gagne.

Canadian Cataloguing in Publication Data

McNeil, Florence
    Breathing each other's air

ISBN 0-919591-87-9
I. Title.
PS8575.N43B7 1994   C813'.54   C94-910124-9
PR9199.3.M26B7 1994

Florence McNeil's Previous Publications

Poetry:
A Silent Green Sky (Klanak, 1967)
Walhachin (Fiddlehead, 1972)
The Rim of the Park (Sono Nis, 1972)
Emily (Clarke, Irwin, 1975)
Ghost Towns (McClelland & Stewart, 1975)
A Balancing Act (McClelland & Stewart, 1979)
The Overlanders (Thistledown, 1982)
Barkerville (Thistledown, 1982)
Swimming Out of History: Poems, Selected and New (Oolichan, 1991)

Juvenile and Young Adult Fiction:
Miss P and Me (Clarke, Irwin, 1982)
All Kinds of Magic (Groundwood, Douglas & McIntyre, 1984)
Catriona's Island (Groundwood, 1988)

Drama:
Barkerville: A Play for Voices (CBC Radio)
Barkerville (New Play Centre)

Non-fiction:
When Is A Poem (ideas for teaching poetry) (League of Canadian
     Poets, 1980)

Work as Editor:
Here Is A Poem: An Anthology of Canadian Poetry (League of
     Canadian Poets, 1983)
*Do The Whales Jump At Night: An Anthology of Canadian Poetry for
     Children* (Groundwood, 1990)

For David, with love

After great pain a formal feeling comes—
The nerves sit ceremoniously like tombs;
The stiff heart questions—was it He that Bore?
And yesterday—or centuries before?

The feet mechanical go round
A wooden way,
Of ground or air of Ought,
Regardless grown;
A quartz contentment like a stone.

This is the hour of lead
Remembered if outlived
As freezing persons recollect
The snow—
First chill, then stupor, then
The letting go.

—Emily Dickinson

PROLOGUE

NOTHING IS HOLDING STILL.

But of course underwater that's what you expected. Great transparent whips moving sideways, and your mouth full of seaweed. I'm feeling choked, she thinks, stifled. She is squirming under the thrust of water, she can feel her head moving from side to side. Denying this. It isn't supposed to go this way.

But maybe it is. Why should it be different for her?

She feels hands reaching out of the seaweed. Bulbous and brown, more fronds, the kind she used to pop as a child, in the rocky sand in front of her house, their house. Except these hands look larger, have softened into tenderness.

Everything under here moves in waves, like heat hazes on a highway, curious fish swarm around to watch me die, she is saying this to herself. And yet there will be others to join.

She is relaxing, there are words reaching her through the hood, the mask, the breathing tubes, no longer are women relegated to roles merely as pretty diving partners, more and more they are breaking down the barriers...from the *Scuba Diver's Bible*, she sees the words, sees the footnotes, but then her life has been a series of footnotes, and so many words...and now the words turn into bubbles, are lost, and she is wavering again, moving up now, and the evidence is in her head. In the ship that was broken apart.

Or it was.

Or was it even important?

"Then the letting go."

I'm here, she thinks, pieces of me, with pieces of the *Anabelle*. And the other pieces, the other boat, has turned itself into water forms, and floated out of everyone's imagination.

∾

There is a light, but it is dim, the light filtered through swarms of sea bloom, of tiny fish, of waving dark plants.

There are arms which hold her head, cradle her body.

There is a voice, and she is floating on its sounds. And machines that whir like a drowning engine.

She is conscious of a face, familiar and yet not familiar, in waves. She is having a migraine, she thinks, and then she makes out someone in white watching her, there has been darkness, there is a light, faces from the dark, light and dark, Easter vigil, but this face is set, set against a curving ceiling—she is in a tomb…there are two people in white now, a man and a woman, they have come closer. She hears them say she is conscious.

∾

She drifts back into the ocean…

1

The mountains were dividing themselves, layer upon layer. Surfaces that crept down submerging themselves somewhere out of sight. Out of her vision.

This is what removed Calgary—the plains, the yellow summers, the white winters—from the coast. The colours of the coast were blue and green—the trees sometimes bluer than the ocean, the ocean taking on the deep, clotted green of the forests. In distance under one thousand miles, in reality moving from ranchland to rain forest, from desert to water.

The car is turning now, angling steeply, a last precipitous descent, leaving behind the white crags of mountains. Beyond—the flat, green checkerboards of line, and the first glimpse of ocean.

Coming home. And immediately, the voices in her head. In the straight, flat plain, truths became obvious; philosophers, she had been told, prefer deserts. The snap of ocean scent, the ebullient tangle of trees, familiar as the lineaments of a dream, the floating landscapes that have come back move now into her consciousness.

❦

Richard Baxter is as dapper as ever; he has lived most of his life in England, and has a curious overlay of Oxbridge upon underlying Canadian, the mid-Atlantic liquidity of the early CBC radio announcers that is impossible to pin down.

"Elizabeth." He stands up behind his desk, he holds out his hand, it is soft, his nails impeccably manicured; she feels like hiding her own ragged cuticles, the nails bitten to the quick. "How good to see you."

May is coming in through the window. West coast May, swirling with lilacs, roses, flagrant green. "I'd forgotten how beautiful this campus is."

"Gorgeous—Lotus Land, indeed."

She pulls over a small armchair and deliberately places it beside his desk, sensing his discomfort and staying there anyway. She knows Richard likes people at a distance.

A shaft of light catches a glass paperweight, subtle rainbows are emerging.

"You're settled in your apartment? Yes? Is it suitable?"

"Very. Thanks for arranging it. I understand apartments are at a premium out here."

"Everything in housing has become insane." He folds his hands in a gesture that looks almost prayerful. "So...and you're away on another book...biography this time. I don't know your subject."

"A woman I discovered when I was looking over material on the Klondike gold rush. She owned a saloon, married three times, bought up half the Yukon and ended up on the stage and in silent films, at the very beginning of films. I've written most of it, I'm not satisfied with the ending."

"My God." There is a slight disapproval in Richard's tone—Ursula would not be a woman who would find favour with him. He carefully places his gold Cross pen and pencil in their velvet box.

"Fascinating woman. Quite influential, in her time."

"Lived out here?"

"Died out here. Rather mysteriously."

"Really? By the way, Elizabeth, would you like a spot of lunch?" He is glancing at his watch. Rolex, gold.

"I'd like that, Richard."

The sun is glorious, blue sky swirling through dotted leaves, the mountains soaring. Inter-session classes have begun, and students in shorts and bright shirts walk or loll on the grass.

Richard is exactly right here. The Faculty Club is deferential, leather, Persian, soft. He sits across from her and smiles; he has made himself up, but his smile is nice. His blazer impeccably cut; on his tie, tiny rowers frozen in oceans of blue silk.

Elizabeth's salad is crisp and filled with shrimp, prawns, crab, the wine cool. She feels like kicking off her shoes and stretching back.

"And so, how's everything at the U. in Calgary?"

"The same. Same old gripes, everyone's still there, though, hanging on; you're the only one who's left the department in the last few years."

"Ah well, one doesn't dare, nowadays." The dessert trolley has stopped at their table. Over his own protestations, Richard chooses a strawberry shortcake, Elizabeth picks out something frosty and glacé.

"I certainly could use more people, Elizabeth, History 101 is completely out of control, amphitheatres of students, it's not sensible."

Elizabeth fluffs the table napkin over her white pants—she is not good at runny desserts. "It's the same everywhere. I have a first year class, enormous—I do have an assistant, though."

"What I'd like to do is pry you loose from there, Elizabeth. I'd love to have you in this department. And you've got Canadian/American history which we could use more of—certainly the most important field..."

Liar, thinks Elizabeth. From your medieval viewpoint, Richard, you hardly know there's history in these here colonies. He was neatly spooning up whipped cream and icing. Richard was neat. Like her mother. Damn, I should phone her, thinks Elizabeth, and is annoyed at herself for thinking that. *Should*. They form a title, her mother's name followed by should.

"Would you like to come back to the campus, Elizabeth?" Richard's smile is professional now. "Would you like to teach here? It would be a coup to get you…you're making quite a name for yourself." She wonders if he's serious.

"Honestly, I don't know. It's beautiful…"

"…and home."

"Well, it was…"

A colleague of Richard's, a burly man who smells of sweet cigars and is wearing blue jeans and a thick sweater, has stopped at the table. She is introduced. It is warming, a small insect is buzzing at the empty dessert plates. Elizabeth glances through the long windows—two cats, one extremely pregnant, are sitting outside.

Elizabeth remembers the cats outside the Graduate centre when she was a student—university cats, plump and tame, who sequestered in stair niches when the rains came.

∾

The stone steps reach from the Gothic stone library, are at once frightening and inviting, or that was what Elizabeth had felt as a student in her first year at this University. The building was overpowering; at seventeen she stood in awe staring up at the stained glass windows, with the light streaming through as if from a projector. The silence, strangled sounds, steps, chairs scraping, low voices, and the sense of all that was carried behind the counters and doors, all that she didn't know, could never know. Like the ocean, lines without boundaries. Limitless.

She had come from a small girls' school on the outskirts of Vancouver, a school that had drifted out to Cedarglen, cut off from the lush private schools of Vancouver's west side, an anachronism, perched looking down at the Second Narrows bridge, at the working inlet in a working man's district. Looking at tugboats and grain ships. Not the postcard expanse on the other side of town, an idle ocean catering to sailboats and motor yachts.

Ursula's yacht. The *Anabelle*.

McKay, Eliza, born May 10, 1870, Glengarry, Ontario, died, October 29, 1915, in Vancouver, B.C. Lived in Montreal, San Francisco, New York, Dawson City, London, Paris. Marchioness of Derbyshire, Mrs. Raymond J. Cunningham III, performed on stage under name of Ursula La Fontaine, pioneer actress, investor, early motion pictures, stage, made famous such roles as Joan of Arc, Elizabeth of Hungary. Her endowments to the world of pioneer film and her enthusiastic championing of this new art form are among the greatest early contributions to the cinema.

⥲

In the special collections, in the Northwest Room, photographs of Ursula La Fontaine. One taken sideways, she looking coyly over her shoulder, one hand on a small table with fluted legs. She is striking, not beautiful, her hair piled up so tightly the effect is of a short hair cut, she has penetrating eyes, a smile which is barely there, her mouth turned up slightly in the manner of an oriental cat, predetermined, set, her figure robust in the style of the day, amplified with frills; she is described in contemporary reports as spirited and chameleon-like. Her pose looks temporary, as if she might rush off at any moment to change costumes. To become Ursula as Marie Antoinette, her costume velvet, the hat so enormous it looks as if it might drown her. Or Cleopatra, on a divan, one hand holding a mirror, the other reaching out to catch the butterfly gauze of her skirt. Or Lady Macbeth, covered like a nun, her hand raised in a small conspiratorial gesture, her eyes sideways, evasive, suspicious. All now laughably melodramatic.

In the ancient silent films Elizabeth has seen, Eliza—Ursula—is in constant motion, her gestures grandiose, she fills the screen. Even in a time of histrionic acting, she is extreme, rushing to the edge of dramatized crises, filling up the squares, the dots.

Elizabeth in her nearly two years of research has found boxes of files, envelopes of articles. Ursula used the press well; items were dropped constantly into newspapers, magazines, like pieces in a paper chase. She created, packaged and sold herself in a way that any modern star might envy.

She would not, however, have chosen the last act.

Elizabeth opens another envelope—she had seen much of this material. Ursula as marchioness, regal, unsmiling; the marquis, small, wizened, leaning on an ivory cane. Behind them the doorway of the great home near Bournemouth, in Hampshire, they are standing on stone steps, they are surrounded by ivy, out of the picture the building soars into the sky, huge, square, with elaborate cornices, a procession of urns on steps that roll down to exquisite gardens, a lake, a tuft of trees.

The marquis is her second husband. She was born to subsistence farmers in Glengarry, Ontario and married at seventeen a widower twenty-four years older than she was, who owned a hundred acres of land and a substantial gabled farmhouse. She was to say later, mockingly, the widower was a complete and terrible bore. (Her mother, intelligent, unhappy, had worked in wealthy households in Montreal, and Ursula seems to have decided early that she belonged in such a milieu, but not as a servant). The widower was killed when his horse bolted during an early morning ride; they had been married only two years. Ursula exchanged the large acreage for a small townhouse in Montreal on Ste. Catherine Street, and took in boarders—professional gentlemen: young lawyers, businessmen. The record is not clear; she seems to have been able to move rapidly around the fringes of Montreal society, seen often with wealthy men. Were they paying her for her companionship? Whatever she was doing, she was discreet, and set to make the most of her introduction to the visiting, elderly and extremely wealthy marquis. He was in the new world on a prescribed sea voyage, a curative, for his chronic bronchitis. He arrived on a palatial yacht, two hundred feet long. The picture of the yacht is in the *Montreal Gazette*. Ursula was to say in later years, "Early on, I had an appreciation of the power exerted by owners of large yachts. One day, I decided I would become one of them."

The marquis, of course, will not be here for long. He is already, in this picture, in decline. He is to die of pneumonia, with press reports of Ursula's faithful attendance on him, though throughout the illness, which lasted nearly a month, she is seen at a hunting meet, splendid in a tight black riding costume, a formal ball at a neighbouring great house (tantalizing evidence suggests she was sleeping with a young earl—this liaison seems to have come to nothing), and taking late supper at Claridge's in London. She said throughout her life that it was important for her not to be bored. She is to mourn the passing of the marquis publicly in a decorous funeral procession—horses in black plumes, Ursula in dark, tight mourning clothes, a becoming black veil. To fight discreetly with the family over the inheritance, accepting, quietly, a sum (Elizabeth has not found out the amount), free to become Mrs. Raymond J. Cunningham III, of Fifth Avenue and Newport, with a pied-à-terre in Paris and a villa in the country outside Sienna. (Mr. Cunningham hated Europe—he had acquired these properties in speculative deals; only Ursula visited them.)

There is nothing new here.

Elizabeth has been thinking of the shipwreck. This is what is troubling her, what she has come to Vancouver to explore. The shipwreck she wants to highlight, providing a sensational tragic ending to Ursula's life. The *Anabelle*, Ursula's yacht, sunk October 29, 1915, in Howe Sound, near the entrance to Vancouver harbour, the narrowing inlet surrounded by islands. The story, still persisting, of the *Anabelle*'s deliberate ramming by another ship. The screen directs Elizabeth to a bound volume which the librarian brings out from the back room.

"There's quite a lot on this shipwreck." The librarian looks familiar—Elizabeth wonders if he had been at the university when she was a student. He has a smoker's cough and faded skin.

"There's a fair amount on Ursula La Fontaine, too." She has told him of her project. "I've brought photographs." He hands Elizabeth a box. "We're still sorting."

"Dr. Peterson's collection?"

"You know about that?"

"I was a student here."

"Of course. I'd forgotten that." A breeze blows in through the window jarred out on its old fashioned hinges: cigarettes, coffee, fresh-cut grass, sweet willows and the pervasive undercurrent of ocean. "But yes...of course you were here."

"A long time ago."

"And I was here earlier than that. I think I was born here," he grinned, an unexpectedly mischievous grin on the pallid features. "They'll carry me out of here. I'm a fixture." Elizabeth knew about the fixtures; this university had spawned a plethora of professors emeriti haunting the campus, so old they seemed to have forgotten what they were doing here. Drifting like the leaves, the fragile rain. She remembered her old teacher of first-year Latin who had brought in his own very old teacher for a guest lecture, and the old man had walked immediately to the window, turning to stare into the wet trees, standing in silence for what seemed like an embarrassing length of time. Yet his lecture, when he gave it, was lucid, if not exciting—Caesar and Cicero punctuated with stories of the First World War, his arms in the academic robe raised, crow-like, to emphasize a point.

This is a good place to become embalmed, she thinks—maybe I should come out here. Wither away in comfort. Greg had told her she'd end her days as a gnarled old lady professor.

He'd told her that one day when they were fighting. She is bemused by the thought...*one day*. When were they *not* fighting?

She feels a twinge, and then very deliberately puts Greg out of her mind.

Elizabeth opens the box first. The pictures are of various shipwrecks, many on the west coast of Vancouver Island. She picks through them carefully, there are wounded ships on reefs, on their sides, gaping, their sterns pointed towards the sky, ships broken in half, rotting, some with beached prows, a mast erupting through a boiling sea. She finds it hard to look at them. As a diver, Elizabeth had avoided the wreck dives. Except for the Caribbean dive, but that ship had been tamed, ornamented with coral and pink fish, harmless. She was not sure she wanted to encounter west coast wrecks.

2

IT WAS IN TORONTO, where Elizabeth was a Ph.D. student, that she learned how to dive.

She had felt almost impelled. To see what she was afraid of. Wanting to go under the water which filled her dreams with horrors, trapped in ships that spiralled under, nostrils filling, lungs filling, part of the ocean. The pictures of dying ships, the pictures she studied with shivers of apprehension, knowing which page framed the ships which never returned. Her father in the sea. The lakes would be different, the lakes would be a starting point. She wanted to go under. With her friend, Rhonda, who had been fearful at first, and then saw it as supremely liberating.

"Ted, my husband (she still referred to him as such, even though they had been divorced for years), was scared out of his skull even to wade—" Rhonda was relishing the fact. "This is the last thing he'd ever want me to do." He remained a point of reference.

Elizabeth and Rhonda signed up for a course with the University Underwater Society, and for a set fee of sixty-five dollars got five classroom sessions, six pool dives and the use of the complicated equipment, which to Elizabeth was a source of both fear and amazement.

Being weighed down with wet suit, hood, mask, weight belt, tanks, regulators and gauges, however, abated her fear. They were no longer human, were scientifically equipped to withstand whatever might await.

They proceeded to open water. Three hours from Toronto, where Georgian Bay reached its rocky windswept peninsula into Lake Huron, where in twenty feet of water Elizabeth felt a weightless sense of freedom, which she could not compare to anything she'd known before. The swims in the pool had been bordered, barricaded. In this limitless bay, with its ancient rocks bulging and receding, a moonscape, relentlessly cold so that only on occasion could gloves and hood be dispensed with.

There were many trips to Georgian Bay, occasionally the sighting of splintered fragments that could be bits of wreck— the spit of land had seen battered vessels going down—but the splinters failed to excite Elizabeth. This was not her history, the shipwrecks of central Canada had not touched her life.

3

IN THE BEGINNING, when she had been first drawn to Ursula, she knew nothing of the shipwreck.

She had found Ursula while researching the book on the Klondike: *Guarding the Gold: Canadian and American Territorial Disputes of the Klondike Gold Rush.* (The title for popular appeal, the sub-title for academic respectability.) It was her second book (the first book scarcely counted, a text to go with pictures of both sides of the 49th parallel, *The People Along the Line*), and in its pursuit Elizabeth had visited the Yukon, travelling on the train through the White Pass summit, staying at grubby motels in Whitehorse and Dawson City. Whitehorse was modern frontier, small businesses, hunting and drinking. Dawson City gave her Ursula. Ursula had lived here for a while, owned saloons, a theatre (still in existence); now the town was made over for tourists, but there were photographs and furnishings, rooms of velvet and bearskin, a gaslight stage, trappings of the gold rush era. The flavour Elizabeth wanted for her book.

Much of her Klondike material came from her Ph.D. thesis, but her book when it came out received some good reviews, not only in scholarly journals, but also in the popular press, a fact which delighted her. "Bursting with life, a book that re-creates the tumultuous days of the Klondike gold rush at a time when Americans and Canadians crisscrossed the same territory," said the reviewer in the *Globe and Mail*. Sales overall were respectable, at least in terms of Canadian sales. She had anticipated becoming an associate professor on its strength. But she was passed over. Again. Elizabeth had taught at the same university for eleven years. She was livid at her exclusion, especially as others—men—who came after her and had published less, were quickly promoted.

Ursula would show them. Her biography would be even more popular than the Klondike book. It would be thorough, readable, above all, interesting. Ursula would provide enough sensational material, more exciting than the accumulation of characters and data that added up to the Yukon book, with its overextended canvas (this was suggested by some reviewers). Pursuing one character, especially one like Ursula, was more to Elizabeth's liking.

Elizabeth had found material at first in odd places: books on the history of film in the U.S. and Canada, in an old book written in the thirties called *Pioneer Women* where Ursula was included with political feminists (the word was not often used at that time), a woman doctor, and a scientist. The picture accompanying the story showed Ursula, sensibly dressed in a tailored suit, an enormous hat with a dead bird dangling over her forehead, talking to orphans who were lined up military fashion to receive the great lady. None of these articles mentioned the shipwreck.

It was in *The Canadian Encyclopedia* in a brief entry that she discovered Ursula had drowned.

&

There was a clinker boat. Elizabeth's father built it for her on the shores of the inlet, setting the thick keel on a cradle, moulding the curved boards into a ship. It was a present, twelve feet long, full sail, tiny jib, it soared in the light inlet winds, her father taught her how to sail when she was eighteen, it was a graduation present and her mother hated it.

Her mother did not swim, her mother never saw the world under the sea, but Elizabeth and her father flew along the coastline, stopping by creeks that tumbled down from the mountains, passing the hulls of great abandoned ships at drydock, some built, her father said, in the 1890s, but now hulks, rotting into the Inlet, slowly moving down, down, into the bottom, where they would become planks for fish and lichen and sea creatures who would make homes of them, and then suck the life out of them.

"Your father and that awful boat," her mother's eyes full of sorrow, of reproach, "he should never have built it for you."

It was your boat, Elizabeth. But you didn't stop him that day, Mother...

I'll find him though, I'll find him and others, at the bottom of the ocean, there is peace and contentment.

But he was found.

And if I'm found, she thinks, if I can breathe, if the brown fronds would disentangle themselves.

&

Under the immediate surface of the sea it is not blue, not green, it is the colour of water which is colours blended, sifting, parting like curtains and that was something Elizabeth decided early, and that came from her father as so much had. She was colouring a seascape, looking out from the porch on a hot July day when she was five and the deep blue of her crayon was melting onto the paper. "Sea blue," she had sung (was it part of a song, a Hebridean lament, something she had heard her grandmother—her mother's mother—singing, something which came from her grandmother's strange folded mouth which kept so much to herself), her father stopping by, in his winter hat because there was no summer hat, no straw, no cap, nothing which suggested time away from the seriousness of work. But then in those days, there was little leisure wear, as there was little leisure. Not that her father was serious, but he was like the sea, changeable, quixotic. He came from the Depression, he came from a long line of Scots who— once self-sufficient on their island—were herded into the new world, lyrical sardonic people who seemed to be searching forever for something they had lost. "Not sea blue," he said to Elizabeth, "sea green, sea yellow, sea red." She had looked at him, arms on her hips, confident she could argue with him because he would listen to her seriously. "That's silly, sea couldn't be red or yellow." "It could be," he said, "all colours, because it goes all around the world and touches all the lands which are yellow and red and green and pink and full of sunsets and seashells and crying trees. You open your eyes under water, Lizzie, and you'll see every colour." And he had bought her a small mask like the eye of a cyclops and she had seen, standing with water up to her waist in her bathing suit with the ruffly fringe, and her father holding her, silver and yellow fish and water transparent one minute, silty the next and no colour she could ever name. He had given her books naming the flora and fauna of the west coast ocean. "People could live under the sea, Daddy," she said. She felt she had discovered a great truth, and he told her about the lost kingdoms under the ocean, the kingdom of Tir nan Og, the Celtic dreamland where there is only peace and serenity.

Was that what she was looking for when she took up diving?

When she was small she had thought about telling her mother about the kingdom, but of course she wouldn't have understood. Her father had said that to her, in a tone that was both confidential and mocking: "No, Lizzie, your mother doesn't believe in that kind of world at all. She never would."

She wonders if she stops struggling if she could find that kingdom. And join her father. Because she knows now that in the depth of the ocean, at its deepest recesses, the colours fade into blue and green. She is thinking this and the seaweed fronds, fat and kind, reach out to her again.

❧

The dimensions of the *Anabelle* are listed: one hundred and three feet overall, twenty-eight foot beam, with a draft of twelve feet. Her actual length in the water is eighty-nine feet, the other fifteen feet taken up by a long, graceful prow, so that it resembles the early Empress ships which sailed at the turn of the century out of Vancouver for the Orient, eggshell white, graceful and so delicate and responsive to the sea they were often filled with seasick passengers. Her father had seen the last of the old Empresses, which in their beauty seemed more allied to sail than steam, going out through the narrows in the 1930s. He had been at dock at the CPR pier, then a young deckhand aboard the *Princess Charlotte* which made the long, winding route to Alaska along the coast fjords.

There are too many memories. Elizabeth tries to clear her head, she is opening up a house closed for a long time, with objects lying covered with dust and needing to be put away.

Or thrown out. That's what the counsellor—she refused to call her a therapist—had said. "Let it go. Let it go."

❧

There is a picture showing the *Anabelle* at dock, and she is being beautified, readied by sailors in white, in no identifiable uniform, Ursula's own creation perhaps. There is the *Anabelle* at sea, and a staged picture, Ursula reclining, a Turkish pillow behind her, against the mast, and someone, a man in huge, predatory moustaches is reading, or seems to be reading. Her face is pseudo-tragic. What sort of heroine is she in this picture? The *Anabelle* aft, her bow cluttered with ladies in stiff white dresses sitting in a circle, sitting upright in whalebone, the constriction that keeps them erect, their hats perched on their upswept hair, anchored with huge pins, nothing must rearrange this picture.

Ursula, on her yacht, is never seen wearing a hat.

There is a hazy picture of the *Anabelle* disappearing into a spring mist, though autumn was the time of her disappearance in fact, and a clear, vibrant day, the kind that shows up everything.

And yet nothing. The clarity of the day did not reveal, to Elizabeth's satisfaction, the cause of the collision. The suggestion of enemy agents, the target, the highest ranking Admiral in Canada, struck her as melodramatic and unbelievable.

The history books had softened: "It was thought at the time to be an act of sabotage." But there was no other theory offered.

4

ELIZABETH'S APARTMENT IS CLOSE to the campus; a faculty member overseas for four months—it would be exactly enough time for Elizabeth to complete her book. Her editor was becoming impatient—she had seen chapters, was excited (editors, Elizabeth had discovered, were always excited—it was a trade word). Her borrowed suite is on the eighth floor of a sixties projectile that shoots up from the stuccoed houses around it, the ones Elizabeth remembers. She also remembers the maple and oak trees, part of the many imported and domestic deciduous giants sprinkled throughout Vancouver; few of the native cedars, hemlocks, remained even twenty-five years ago. The view from the tiny balcony, with its chained bicycle, is breathtaking, the mountains very close, as if the landscapers had added them only recently to the scene. (In Calgary, the Chamber of Commerce was fond of painting the city ringed with mountains; in truth, one had to climb very high on a tower to catch glimpses of the cold and aloof Rockies, perpetually snow covered.) There is no snow on these mountains, they are swathed in blue and green, round, and at one time she might have thought friendly.

She has bought a frozen dinner; she puts it in the microwave and tells herself tomorrow she'll stock up on fresh fruits
and vegetables. The kitchen is a galley, sparsely furnished
with glass pots and pans. It faces through a lattice into the
small living room filled with Swedish furniture, the kind you
bring home in crates, bright, hard, and impermanent, looking
as if you could gather it up each night, like children's toys, and
put it away.

The small bedroom has a round bed. There are vapid
sketches of eighteenth century London on the wall. The professor is British, teaches in the English Department, his book-
cases hold a large collection of the writings of Swift, Pope,
Goldsmith. Elizabeth decides she will remove the bland
sketches, put up splashes of Mondrian and Matisse, or whatever she can find that is vibrant and colourful.

Elizabeth feels uncomfortable in the round bed; she prefers to stretch out, and feels in this bed that she should remain
curled up in a fetal position to echo its curves. Nights are still
difficult, it is only two weeks since she has separated from
Greg, she still finds herself longing for the safety of his body
beside her, for their completion.

Then she remembers the fights, the accusations, the apartment become a battleground, the disputes so routine that they
almost seemed choreographed, facing each other in various
squares in the apartment, which because they were using
mostly Greg's furniture, was modernistic: hard, plastic cubes
and angled lights. Her own pieces—overstuffed curved chairs,
a Victorian settee—looked alien and immense among the neat,
geometric designs. They had chosen Greg's apartment because it was larger than hers, it had a view of the river snaking
its way through town, and far away, beyond the world's
highest tower, the jagged Rockies.

The view was not liberating. The apartment—Greg's apartment—not *their* home—held secrets in its beige walls which
Elizabeth could not divine. She felt it was a knowing apartment, containing vestiges of other lives, of people who had
come and gone, who were unknown to Elizabeth, but who

remained watchful. She could not find comfort in it.

Elizabeth and Greg were defined by their differences. Her assertions (said Greg) were tangled, exaggerated, profuse, like the west coast.

Greg was uneasy on trips to the coast. He felt closed in, he said, suffocated—he missed the long view of the prairies, where the dot in the distance suggested a mountain which knew its place.

"You can't *see* on the west coast," he said. "There's too much in the way."

"But that's *how* you see," she said, and he hadn't understood.

She is back at the Northwest Room next morning. "Hi, you're an early bird," the librarian looks away from his computer.

"I'll have the box I was looking at yesterday."

"Ah, the pictures...I found some newspaper clippings, too. Actually there's a *lot* of material on the sinking of the *Anabelle*. It was headline news in 1915."

"What I've found out so far sounds absolutely unbelievable."

"You mean the possibility of sabotage?"

"Yes. It sounds like something out of a spy novel. Were there German boats floating around the coast in 1915?"

"I doubt it. The people accused were British people, of German extraction—I'm trying to think of the name—Hausmann, I think...Apparently inoffensive couple—husband and wife, lived around here somewhere."

"This is my missing link. Putting Ursula to rest. Clearing up the end of her life."

"You've got most of your material then?"

"Yes. Some in the Yukon, in the National Archives in Ottawa, a good deal in New York...at the City Archives. The book is nearly complete. I'm not satisfied with the ending—I need more material on the shipwreck."

"You look chilly, Dr. Morrison...would you like a cup of our potent staff coffee?"

She looks at him gratefully, follows him to a small cluttered enclosure. She had put on a light cotton pants suit forgetting coastal mornings could be so raw. She warms her hands on a mug decorated with seagulls, finishes the coffee quickly, then takes her box to a carrell close to a window; outside a willow empties itself against the paned glass.

The librarian is beside her. "Excuse me, Dr. Morrison, but I've found another box, all of this stuff was together." He hands her a dilapidated wine-coloured box bound with elastic. "Of course, as you knew Dr. Peterson, you knew about the collection."

"He owned the history of Vancouver."

She remembers him in his dotage, a button missing from his vest, dandruff and pipe ashes rearranging his suit, wandering possessively among his boxes and snarling at anyone who suggested cataloguing. She remembered hearing how he disappeared from the boxes, to a nursing home, to repeat interminable snippets of unrelated history to anyone who would listen, eventually only to himself.

The wine–coloured box proves interesting. She finds a newspaper clipping with black headlines:

> *Daily Province*, October 30, 1915 (day)
> Terrible Tragedy at Sea, Mysterious Double Sinking.
> Admiral Drowned.
> Ursula La Fontaine Among Victims.
> Possible Sabotage. Only Cabin Boy Survives.
> *The* Anabelle, *the luxury yacht owned by the actress Ursula La Fontaine, was lost yesterday in Howe Sound, near Anvil Island, with its*

*entire complement of passengers and crew, save
for a cabin boy, still in serious condition.*

*The day was clear, but a wind sprang up, the
famous "Squamish" wind, which can appear
suddenly with deadly force. The cause of the
sinking was, however, an unexplained collision
with a smaller vessel, hitherto unnamed.*

A tug, the Annie B. *captained by William
Swenson, arrived on the scene too late to help.
Capt. Swenson, who states he was about two
miles away, rounding an island, was able only to
witness the scene from a distance. His journey
was made slower by the fact that he had in tow a
large log boom, and was travelling slowly. He
put into a cove on Bowen Island with his boom,
and made for the scene of the sinking. "I heard
this loud noise," he stated. "I knew what was
happening, but I couldn't get there in time."*

*When he arrived at the site of the accident the
two boats were already gone, the wind was
blowing fiercely, and there were no signs of
survivors.*

*"There was wood and chairs, clothing and
debris everywhere but no people. I radioed the
coast guard right away. It must have been some
collision," said Capt. Swenson. "They went down
like they'd been torpedoed."*

*Reporters have so far been unable to speak
with Jim Rowan, fifteen-year-old cabin boy, the
only survivor, now in St. Paul's Hospital, in
grave condition, having been picked up off Anvil
Island, more dead than alive.*

*Searchers and divers have recovered ten bod-
ies, among them the body of the famous actress,
Ursula La Fontaine. There was thought to be a
party of twenty or so aboard the* Anabelle.

Little is known of the occupants of the other

> *boat, except that it is rumoured that they were of German origin. This has given rise to speculation of deliberate ramming of the* Anabelle. *"We are examining all possibilities," said Officer Nigel Branshaw of the Harbour Police. "We have not ruled out an act of sabotage. Admiral Bailey was about to embark for overseas on an undisclosed mission. We cannot comment further."*

A list of the passengers of the *Anabelle* is included. The most notable, other than Ursula and Admiral Alexander Bailey, are a judge, the president of the Bank of California, an American writer of popular western novels, two women (besides Ursula), Mrs. Clarence Styron, the wife of the bank president, and Mrs. Jonathan Truro, the wife of the judge.

Elizabeth suddenly feels great sympathy for the women who went to their deaths without their own names.

Ursula was, as always, the exception.

She had her own name, others' names, and one she invented.

❧

Elizabeth wonders about the tantalizing hints in the article, "the undisclosed mission," "the mysterious double sinking." These statements in themselves would be enough in the fevered days of 1915 to have unleashed a flood of rumours.

There is microfiche material, more newspaper accounts. There was an enquiry; the captain and the crew of the *Anabelle* were exonerated (posthumously); the captain knew every inch of these waters, was a trusted employee of Ursula La Fontaine, was respected, sober, conscientious, had served on several of the CPR boats which went up and down the coast.

The testimony of the cabin boy who came back to life affirmed the ramming of the *Anabelle* by the small boat, whose name, it turned out, was the *White Swan*.

In succeeding newspaper accounts the *White Swan* becomes more and more sinister. A moving iceberg, a missile, a "submarine, " a new word added to the hysterical lexicon of ocean horrors in 1915.

The *White Swan* was captained by Tom Hausmann; his only passenger, his wife Bess. Their bodies were discovered swept up on the north shore of Bowen Island, close together.

Hausmann was a Germanic name—were the couple in the service of the Hun? Was it a suicide ship?

The target was clear: not Ursula, but her guest on the voyage, Admiral Alexander Bailey, the ranking Canadian admiral, instrumental in the formation of the new Canadian Navy, now separated from the parent Royal Navy; home base—Esquimalt, B.C.

Was he to embark on a secret mission? Was he an agent for the Allied Forces? There was much speculation.

5

ELIZABETH IS STILL EATING microwave meals. At the ding she takes out a pseudo-gourmet meal, chicken cordon bleu, which for all its claims looks depressingly like the 1950s' hash of meat, potatoes and apple sauce which her family had greeted with delight when they all sat in front of the new tin TV tables in the semi-dark room staring at the test pattern beneath the ceramic deer. The TV dinners were novelties, brought in only occasionally—her mother did not like her job usurped.

In Cedarglen. The name singularly unimaginative, north of Vancouver, at one time heavily forested, sloping down to the Inlet. The family lived under trees and stared at the ocean, the mountains, it was a view that seemed as necessary, as inevitable, as her mother's astounding array of good suppers and spectacular baked goods. Behind the wine curtains (given to the family by an aunt who had finished with them) was the ocean, so near you could hear it lap, so sheltered it rarely stormed, at its worst looking like froth on the top of cocoa, signalling something was stirring, but nothing of harm.

Her father, her mother, Elizabeth. A threesome from *Ladies Home Journal*, sitting close, mother in apron and moccasin slippers with fur, which now that she was putting on weight seemed too flat to carry her, her father back from his latest job.

Her father's jobs were varied—he was an artist (self-taught) whose sketches, black and white, hurried, framed with unpainted wood, filled the house, a draughtsman who hated the tedious hours in a sterile, tidy office at the draughting table, in particular, Elizabeth remembers, a brief job in mechanical design, drawing pictures, as he put it, of bloody nuts and bolts. He had worked in all three of Cedarglen's hardware/lumber stores: clerk, truck driver, stock filler. The latest job was always the solution, the answer (to what, Elizabeth now wondered—to her father's dissatisfactions? her mother's urgent proddings?). The finances were looked after by her mother, whose balancing of the books was set up with rigid ceremony: the insertion of a nib into the tapering pen (her mother always used ink—brave girl, her father said), the squat blue ink bottle, the blotter, the ink eraser (never used) beside her on the kitchen table. If a mistake were made—infrequently—it was carefully crossed out, Elizabeth watching her mother's small, efficient fingers attacking the offending figure. Though her mother seemed to enjoy the accounting, there was always an indefinable chill, a lowering, which filled the room when the ritual began. It was as if her mother expected some day to look up from the book to announce that the family was finished, going under, swallowed up.

It never happened. They always squeaked by. Her father's words, which he would address to her mother: "You worry too much, Maggie, we always squeak by." Her mother assuming the look of patient martyrdom which Elizabeth had come to expect. At those times, watching her mother watch her father, Elizabeth hated her mother.

❧

Ursula in Dawson City: there, the photographs are even more blurred; it is as if they are taken always through a haze of snow, even indoors. Ursula behind a wooden bar, in the background a huge mirror, beside her the bartender in a black suit. She is much smaller than he is, she is looking up, sideways at him, but it is clear even through the dots, the wash of time, that he is in her thrall. His posture is deferential, frozen in submission.

In actuality, there are few pictures of Ursula with men. She is mostly alone, swathed in furs—in one photograph, standing by a sleigh and dog team. Is she about to travel? If there is a man standing by, he is not visible. Ursula did not make that kind of mistake.

She has come to the Yukon from San Francisco, she has become an actress with, it seems, the blessing of her husband, the wealthy stockbroker, J. Raymond Cunningham, who was an unorthodox scion of a staid family, who had a florid tenor voice, specialized in arias and songs made famous by Caruso, and in his twenties had travelled briefly with a second-rate vaudeville show. He was enamoured of the theatrical life and excessively proud of his wife's talent.

He was also an alcoholic and frequently out of the picture.

He is to disappear completely, confined to a lunatic asylum on the outskirts of New York, leaving Ursula free to take "The Troupe La Fontaine" on the road. And to translate it ultimately into "La Fontaine Films" with a studio in a large New York warehouse. Hollywood had not yet been invented.

From then on men do not enter her pictures. Her disdain for them was complete.

6

AFTER DINNER, AT TELEVISION TIME, there would be a time for the approximation of the magazine family ("Never Underestimate the Power of a Woman"; "Survival in the Suburbs"): her mother bringing three cups of tea (with saucers—never mugs), setting them on the wobbly TV tables; her father, washed, a fresh ironed shirt with rolled-up sleeves, plaid slippers, renewed after her mother's always sumptuous supper, the lines eased, flicking ashes into the tall smoke stand. Elizabeth in jeans with turned-up cuffs, long plaid shirt, and the TV taking away the need to speak. Meaning there was someone to cue you for laughter, a release. When it was over, and darker, the curtains stayed closed and the ocean slept.

There was something missing...there was always something missing. Elizabeth cannot remember seeing her parents embrace, except once at Christmas, for a photograph. It was staged, their arms entwined, looking like cardboard pictures at a fair—real heads, paper bodies.

Her mother was no match for her father. In any sense of the word.

"She isn't like you, Lizzie," he said more than once, always with a laugh, "she's very practical—." The word was an implied criticism, heavily underlined.

Why had her father ever married her mother?

Elizabeth's grandmother had said once that her mother was very attractive, sweet, and serene." An anchor for your father," she had said.

She had also, Elizabeth found out later, been three months pregnant. In those days that meant the decision was made for you.

Yes, certainly her mother came out of TV-land, or a book, a movie, a reader, even. Dick and Jane's mother, whose pink hands moved from page to page preparing soups and lunches and whose red mouth said nothing of interest.

Run Mother run.

I should phone her, thinks Elizabeth.

Not yet.

7

ELIZABETH IS STILL DIGGING in Dr. Peterson's box. At the bottom of the box she finds a leather account book, the edges are peppered with mould and ragged with what looks like the marks of fire. She opens it gingerly; the first page is entitled "Bess Hausmann: Household Accounts," and she realizes she is holding the records of the woman, accused with her husband, of sabotage.

The pages are not entirely clear—there are water marks amid the mould but she can decipher most of it.

Bess has listed everything, all in categories: food, garden supplies, household staples—and then a long category entitled Tom's Expenses. Tom had subscriptions to the *Gentleman's Omnibus, The Times of London, Punch, The Sportsman's Quarterly*; he seemed in need of large quantities of The Smoker's Friend Tobacco, port, and brandy. And then there was the boat. Elizabeth follows its history through the faded pages: oak planks, caulking, fouling paint, brass. It is clear a large portion of the Hausmann budget is directed toward Tom's boat.

Elizabeth takes off her glasses and wipes her eyes; she is

developing allergies. ("It's the damp out here—it will all come back," her mother warning her.)

Elizabeth carefully turns pages. It is an ordinary household account book, but very thorough—Bess Hausmann was a painstaking record-keeper. She also seemed to have spent remarkably little on herself. Occasionally an item appears: under clothing, for instance, after the mackintosh seaman's sweater and rubber boots for Tom, there is a bolt of cotton, ninety cents from Eaton's catalogue. A few other items—Pears Shampoo, Vaseline Lip Balm. These were probably shared items.

Elizabeth stares out at the deep sunny grass, at the students in their day-glo colours, and feels annoyed by Bess, the careful wife.

She closes the book and puts it back.

There are no records of secret missives, furtive telegraphs. But of course there wouldn't be.

Only the accounting of a woman whose place in society was predetermined, the faithful and loyal helpmate, second in command. (Never first.)

Elizabeth tells herself she must be careful not to make up a character—not to read too much into the record. She decides to get some fresh air, walks along the willow-encircled path; in front of her, a boy and a girl. The boy brushes the girl's hand briefly, she smiles at him, their bodies are edging together. They seem to Elizabeth like sea creatures trapped in an aquarium.

Elizabeth feels suddenly tired, depressed. She has moved back, come full circle, and cannot comprehend it.

8

THE LIBRARIAN HAS NEWS FOR HER.

"I thought you'd be interested, Dr. Morrison. A Ph.D. candidate—in history—was in here looking for material—political material, really—but he asked me, incidentally, if I had a picture of the *Anabelle*. Turns out he and some friends are divers and they intend to dive on the *Anabelle*."

"Really...?"

"You don't dive, do you?"

"Yes, actually I do. I haven't this year so far..."

"The student is Paul Allenberg. You can probably reach him at the history department. I thought you'd be interested."

"I am. Very."

The librarian asks her to have lunch with him. His name is Will Beaton. They eat at the faculty club; the day has warmed—Will looks uncomfortable in his tweed jacket with the unfashionable lapels.

"I mostly eat out," he tells her. "I'm getting used to being an old bachelor." She discovers his wife died of lung cancer two years ago.

"I'm nearly ready to retire—we were planning to go on a

world cruise..." His eyes are pale watery blue, hair pepper and salt grey, his face grey also...she remembers her father's face grey like that after exertion. In the later years.

"Is your family here? " he asks her.

"My mother lives just outside of Vancouver. My father's dead."

"Oh."

He glances at her left hand; she is not wearing a wedding ring. But he does not comment. Not that wearing a ring would mean anything now. At the time of her marriage it was something Elizabeth showed off, proudly; her colleague, Norah, who had an office next door which she filled with the smoke of long thin cigars, had told her the ring was a badge of captivity. Elizabeth said she didn't care; Greg was wearing one, too.

Her finger has narrowed where the thick ring rested for six years.

Norah was also the one who had mentioned the counsellor, a friend of hers who, according to Norah, "understood women's problems."

Elizabeth and Will both order a sole dish, they both sip Earl Grey tea. "I'm trying to give up cigarettes," Will is saying, his hand holding his cup is shaking. "I know they're terrible for me. But it's an awful habit to break."

After the sole, with its delicate basil sauce, Will asks her about Ursula.

"Quite a woman. Don't get me started."

But he does and she sketches Ursula for him, finding herself concentrating on the detour of the sinking.

"I'm probably babbling," she says. "Ursula has got to me. I have so much material...maybe too much. Discovering more about the shipwreck is putting the cap on everything, completing her life."

"The sinking of the *Anabelle* has taken on a rather mythic quality. You've no doubt heard the tale of the letter supposedly found, mostly illegible, from one of the hands, a quickly scribbled note which washed upon the shore...saying "I love you, all is lost" to his sweetheart." (Elizabeth likes the old-fashioned sound of the word).

"Has anybody seen the note?"

"No, and I doubt it ever happened. If the sinking occurred as quickly as it is reported, he'd never have had time. Romantic story."

His smile is almost wistful and she thinks of the world cruise that had ended.

"Romantic stories abound when it comes to the sea. Like the Titanic, I suppose, stories of supreme courage, the band playing when the ship went down, and the superior bravery of the upper classes—I always wondered why they were depicted as so much braver than the lower classes who behaved like stampeding elephants, it seems, and the wives who stayed with their husbands."

"A good many did. But I know what you mean, it becomes impossible to separate fact from fiction."

She nods. "Everything painted larger than life. A silent movie."

"Have you seen any movies that your Ursula made? They must be incredibly ancient."

"I have. They are. She was very grand, very melodramatic. Probably the worst kind of overacting."

"Then maybe it's fitting she had a dramatic death."

"Yes, I suppose so...*too* dramatic. It's hard to countenance the enemy agents stories. Spy ship on the coast."

"It wasn't at that time. People believed all sorts of things. Look at the newspaper accounts of the war in Europe—the Hun crucifying Belgian soldiers to barn doors, raping women and butchering children. This story—the *Anabelle*—really struck fear into the hearts of Vancouverites, apparently. If there was one ship lurking in the harbour, there might be others."

"But the Hausmanns weren't from Germany—they were British, small farmers living somewhere outside the city."

"That doesn't matter. Look at the Japanese-Canadians in World War II, the way they were herded into camps—war does things like that. You have to create enemies and then go on to paint a whole race as the personification of evil incarnate. That way you can put God on your side." Will sipped slowly at his water glass. "How else would you get people to fight?"

"I know I'm bothered, and, I think out of proportion, by the ending of Ursula's life. It's actually a small percentage of the book, but..." She shook her head.

"It must be hard not to get off into tangents when you're researching."

"Is it ever. Speaking of that—I found Bess Hausmann's account book—in pretty bad shape."

"*Really*? I should go through those boxes again; things are in danger of falling to pieces. We had a pipe break in here a few years ago, and extensive water damage—we had to throw out some of Peterson's boxes; they were beyond repair. We sent off dozens of old books to Texas, if you can imagine, to have them restored."

"I wonder where they or she, or he, or whoever—found the account book. Not underwater, clearly."

"God only knows. The way Peterson kept everything, there is hardly ever a record. I heard that the powers that be had the Hausmann cottage torn down, egged on by an angry crowd, it appears, who helped torch it. Perhaps somebody discovered it at the time, or after."

"Maybe so."

✄

If the hands, the brown fronds, would stop reaching for her, even in their kindly intentions, she would not feel so suffocated...under the sea it is a forest, she thinks, the rain forest looks like this, there was a hike through a forest with Greg perhaps or was it her father with trees thirty stories high and trunks misted with winding moss and the wind howling like the water is howling now and she thinks it shouldn't happen like this.

Or maybe it isn't happening.

9

ELIZABETH PHONING HER MOTHER. The sad voice pulling her backwards.

"Come out soon, Lizzie."

"I will, mother, as soon as I get settled." (As soon as I can steel myself against the questions about Greg and settle the guilt I will feel because Greg is so nice Greg is your husband poor Greg.)

She drives out to Cedarglen, the hill her family had lived on. She is driving through the main street, the main shopping area, and then realizes it no longer is. There are now three malls, her mother has told her...business on Inlet Street is dying. And yet even though some of the old square low buildings with their look of impermanence have disappeared, there are still enough signs for her to remember. She notices a building which is now sporting a cottage-look-alike bay window, travel posters hang in the windows, *Britain in the Summertime*, but above the travel posters, letters fading, Cedarglen Five and Dime. She had come here with her mother, at Christmas, with fifty cents to buy her grandmother glass bowls, or maybe an amber glass vase, to buy her father Yardley shaving cream with the ship on it, to pick out, when her mother turned decorously aside, hankies for her mother or a box of Multiflora talcum powder. At those times she felt closer to her mother; they were conspirators in the great secrets of Christmas, they were also female, and thus understood dishes and hankies and pretty earrings and perfume.

Sometimes, while her mother collected groceries from the Red and White store, Elizabeth dropped in to see her father. She had felt, when she was very small, that he must own the hardware store, or at least have been the inventor and builder of the intricate systems of boxes and bins which held the bolts and nails, screws and fasteners. She was astounded that her father would know all he knew about these things: their varying sizes, their exact purposes. It seemed to her far more incredible than her mother's mixing of flour and milk, butter and baking powder, to produce something which rose amazingly in the oven, became cohesive and identifiable—a cake, a pie, tea scones. That was of passing interest. Her father's knowledge seemed encyclopedic.

As she grew older, she knew his role in the store (whichever one he was in at the time) to be minimal, would sometimes find him standing, slumped against the wall, arms folded, face a mask of boredom. "Get me an Oh Henry, Lizzie," (his favourite snack) he would tell her. By the time she came back from the confectionery store, he might be busy again, with a customer, his face alight with interest, geniality, or moving as he always did in quick, intense bursts of energy, along the cluttered aisles, to some destination or solution.

∾⟨

Her mother's house is not near the ocean—it is perched on a hill, but the mountains still stare at it.

Her mother is getting smaller, grey mingled liberally

through her hair, amid strands that have turned yellow from perming. She hugs Elizabeth who feels like a stick in her mother's encircling embrace. Her mother has forgotten to take her apron off. Elizabeth feels like crying.

Her mother's husband (they have been married ten years) is in the garden; he is a retired barber who had been pampered and scolded into inefficiency by his late wife. He loves the garden, her mother's cooking. He is full of vague sighs and aches, he rejoices in the number of pills he takes. (Elizabeth hears this story each time she visits. Elizabeth dislikes him intensely.)

They have roast beef, roast potatoes, gravy. Jello and whipping cream. Her mother has made no concessions to Lite Eating.

Her husband excuses himself after dinner. He must cover the half-grown lettuce—the slugs are out in full force.

Elizabeth and her mother facing each other in the unrecognizable living room. Only one armchair is familiar; it had been her father's favourite; it is now re-upholstered in striped chenille.

Elizabeth to her mother: "You're keeping well, Mother?"

Her mother: "Yes, thank God, I can't complain. You're looking a bit tired, Lizzie. And skinny. Are you taking care of yourself?"

Elizabeth: "Yes. I'm fine. Busy."

Her mother: "And how is everything else?" The mouth pursed slightly. Blame folded in.

You mean Greg, Mother, Greg is fine, he doesn't really want this separation, Mother, and I'm not sure how it happened, but we were yelling at each other, and I was packing up. Strange, that—doesn't the woman usually stay in the house (apartment in this case)?—but that's the domestic woman who suddenly after twenty years of raising children, and kissing the feet of her man finds out he's having an affair with the office floozy and now wants his freedom to find himself and have more affairs with women who are always young, willing and confused. But it wasn't that way. Greg didn't cheat; neither did I.

Then, as her mother had asked her once—the voice filled with barely disguised indignation—what could Greg have done to you?

See these seaweed whips around my neck, Mother? The ones that are tightening. The kindly fronds. Don't ask me what Greg did. Whatever he did I let him do it. I put on the diving outfit willingly, and he sent me down, and then he cut off the air.

Good night, Mother.

10

ELIZABETH IS ON HER WAY to Victoria.

There is a long line-up at the ferry, many American licence plates, tourists taking pictures of themselves against the ferry backdrop, against rotting stumps, against great soaring cedars. May is turning into June. It is going to be warm, pink and gold is spreading across the sky; the air is still.

The ferry is filled to capacity and she has to park on the middle level. She locks the car, grabs her cotton jacket and walks upstairs slowly, jammed by crowds. She heads out to the deck, takes a deep breath, filling her lungs with the pungent smell of ocean. It has been years since she'd taken this ferry; her clearest remembrance of it was her first trip, with her father and mother. Only it hadn't been this ferry, not a crowded car ferry but the slower, more graceful CPR boat which moved majestically over the water, and lunch served on linen table cloths on real china.

They had tea at the Empress, took a sight-seeing coach around Victoria, bought toffee and chocolates, and returned home slowly, on the night boat, the islands darkening, the sea full of flickering lights from ships that moved like serpents in the dark.

Elizabeth at the ship's railing is staring at the islands, trying to remember which one is which—Galiano, Saturna, Pender—she can't remember. The ferry, moving quickly over the smooth ocean, is leaving a wake; there are seagulls screaming, flying sideways. She puts on her jacket—there is still shadow on the deck.

A man and woman train binoculars on an island that seems near enough to touch; the ship now slithers through the passage.

"It's a bald eagle," the woman is yelling.

"Look at the logging—damn shame," the man says. A straight bare swath cuts the apex of a small hill. It looks odd, a monk's tonsure amid the thick greenery. Everywhere there are these new patches, a mange. She feels suddenly outraged and protective.

Near the island, a dive flag perched on a red buoy bobs in the waves; a dive boat is waiting.

Elizabeth has a sudden longing to dive—it is perhaps time now. She is ready for the west coast ocean.

◈

Elizabeth drives into Victoria, noting how the pretty hills with their oaks frozen into contorted shapes are disappearing, built over with the same small shopping centres, the same suburban tracts one witnesses anywhere.

She parks in the lot adjoining the Empress Hotel; it is very warm now, tourists are being disgorged from the *Princess Marguerite*, the old coastal boat now a summer novelty, her smoke stacks desecrated with a gaudy Union Jack; she looks all wrong, like a sophisticated matron in a dark suit, wearing a silly party hat.

Float planes are also emitting tourists, they are taking

pictures of each other against flower-decked lampposts, against the *Princess Marguerite*, against the tallyho cabs.

Victoria has thoroughly disguised itself—the real colonels and their cricket grounds are gone; now cartoons have been brought in, old English façades, costumed beefeaters, wenches, pseudo-pearlies. Somewhere behind the cartoons there is west coast timber and real people. But they are buried now.

Elizabeth feels hungry and dispirited—obviously summer isn't the best time to visit Victoria.

∽

The archives are housed on the first floor of a solemn stone building. It has soaring arches, steel bars crisscross overhead. There are open windows but the rooms seem airless.

The enquiry proceedings are not on microfiche but bound in a typewritten volume of sessional papers.

The volume is enormous.

It is entitled "An Enquiry into the Sinking of the Yacht, *Anabelle*, Oct 29, 1915. (Why, thinks Elizabeth, is the *White Swan* not even mentioned?) Judge Alexander McIntosh presiding, assisted by Captain Ian J. Farquarson, Wreck Commissioner for British Columbia."

The *Anabelle* is described as a luxury steamer, the salons of the finest teak 'tween decks resembling a palatial—if small— sitting room. Built at Fairfield Shipbuilding works, 1901, for Prince Michael of Hungary who kept it for his visits (frequent) to Britain. On board he entertained royalty, cruised the Mediterranean, took part in races. He took it on only one deep-sea voyage, a very long one which ended up by way of the Horn in British Columbia; the sixty-day voyage, with the relatively small yacht pounded by the high seas, proved to be too much for Prince Michael, who disposed of the *Anabelle* in Vancouver and returned home via the transcontinental train and a very large ocean liner.

The new buyer is, of course, Ursula La Fontaine, who used it for summer vacationing, moving from Vancouver down the coast to California, having just leased a studio for La Fontaine Films; she spent a good deal of time in Vancouver, feeling, she said, "the need to be rooted in Canada." She was not a true Vancouverite, not a property owner, preferring to rent, perhaps a large house in the west end or Shaughnessy, or sometimes commandeering the royal suite at the Vancouver Hotel. She entertained constantly; the Vancouver *Daily Province* printed the names of her guests, the who's who of British Columbia gentry, plus the visiting celebrities and dignitaries.

Judge Alexander McIntosh had begun the proceedings with this statement:

> *Since, unhappily, there is but a single survivor of this disaster, a young boy, who by virtue of a severe concussion is only now able to comment on the last minutes of the ship, it will be very difficult for this enquiry to elicit all the facts which brought about the great tragedy in which some of our most eminent people including Admiral Bailey and Mrs. Raymond J. Cunningham, known also as Ursula La Fontaine, have lost their lives.*
>
> *We have, of course, the testimony of Capt. William Swenson, master of the tug, Annie B., who did not witness the moments before the sinking, arriving only when the ships were in their death plunges. We will proceed.*

The testimony of the cabin boy Jim Rowan, who dictates from his hospital bed:

> *We were cruising up around Howe Sound, past Bowen Island; I was below deck helping the cook. I wasn't what you'd call a regular cabin*

boy—not like I would be on a large ship, where you stick to your own line of work. I was given all kinds of things to do, from swabbing and tidying to running errands for the passengers, and helping the cook. I remember the cook grumbling because he was trying to prepare something for dinner—we were working on one of those jellied salads, and the boat was shaking around something awful, because the storm had just come up. The galley was pretty well prepared for storms—it was the most up-to-date kind of kitchen with everything fitting neatly in place, with rims and edges so things didn't slide off. But I guess jellied dishes are pretty tricky. You know, I helped in the galley so much that I was wondering if I might take up being a cook— a real chef.

I remember I was just washing up a big glass bowl, when all of a sudden there was this terrible crash—wood on wood, I knew the sound, having been in a passenger boat going to Victoria once, that crashed into a dock—no harm done in that one.

The cook he starts yelling bloody murder, and we both of us start heading up the stairs and right then the water started coming in, it was terrible, everyone screaming and running around, and what I remember even through the confusion was Miss La Fontaine, standing at the rail staring at the little boat that was going down, like she didn't know what was happening, and a man and woman trying to climb up on the little boat, and the woman glancing at Miss La Fontaine, and it was like they were both looking at each other just for a second—it's hard to describe but I'll never forget that, never.

And that's all I remember, because there was

this great wrench, like the whole world was
falling in on itself, and I don't know — they tell
me something hit me on the head, and I was
knocked out, and how I got to shore — on Anvil
Island where they found me — I'll never know.
All I remember is that I woke up in this hospital,
and there was these nurses bending over me.

He is asked for other details, all his testimony points to guilt on the part of the small boat, he is sure the small boat was off course, was heading right for the *Anabelle* so that it must have hit her amidships. He knew the captain of the *Anabelle* to be a sober, conscientious man who worked regularly for Ursula La Fontaine, who knew the coast like the back of his hand; he was on course, in spite of the storm. The cabin boy has given this story before, to military naval personnel who came to see him in the hospital and have been very kind to him, and to the press. He has become a hero—the headlines have screamed, "Cabin Boy sole survivor in horrible tragedy"; "Cabin Boy indicts small boat." Sub-heading: "Espionage suspected in sinking of *Anabelle*."

The occupants of the *White Swan* are identified as Tom and Bess Hausmann.

It is, according to a neighbour, their first voyage in the thirty–foot boat which Hausmann had built by hand. The neighbour, Mr. George Blackwell, testifies that the boat was sufficiently seaworthy and that Tom Hausmann had some experience at sea, though only in very small craft. He says Mr. Hausmann was conscientious and sober. He admits that his inexperience in the small boat might have been a causative factor of the accident.

George Blackwell says he had been asked by Tom Hausmann to accompany him on the maiden voyage of the *White Swan*.

"They treated it like they were launching the *Empress of Canada*," he says. He had been unable to go with Hausmann, so Mrs. Hausmann made the decision that she would accompany her husband. It was a shake-down cruise, they were setting out on Burrard Inlet and would go to its mouth and maybe further. They had been in high spirits the night before the launching; they had in fact bought a bottle of champagne to send their boat down the ways. (There was some speculation and questioning at this point: was Mr. Blackwell sure that the occupants of the boat had not indeed been celebrating before they set sail?)

> *They were very responsible people.*
> *But you weren't with them when they left.*
> *No, as I said, I had an appointment in the city*
> *which I could not break.*
> *So you can't be sure.*
> *I know what kind of people they were.*

The line of questioning, of innuendo, starts to unfold. The owners of the small boat had a German name. Is it not possible that they could be in the employ of the Germans—their target the removal of the highest ranking naval officer in Canada?

Mr. Blackwell expresses horror:

> *They were patriotic English people—Tom's*
> *greatest desire had been to go home to England*
> *to serve, but his health wasn't good enough. He*
> *had hoped to offer his boat, the* White Swan, *for*
> *use in the war effort, in whatever capacity the*
> *forces might see fit. He was a model husband,*
> *citizen.*
>
> *And his wife?*
>
> *A totally devoted wife. Her whole life was*
> *given over to the creation of a home. She was*
> *extremely solicitous of her husband whose health*
> *was not of the best...*
>
> *Ah, but many a spy masquerades under the*
> *guise of a patriot.*
>
> *They could not have been spies.*

Have you known any spies, Mr. Blackwell?
No, but—
Then how can you say with authority they
    were not spies?

(The newspapers: "Sabotage suspected in ramming of *Anabelle*.")

The inquest could not of course state categorically that the Hausmanns were spies, but it was enough that there was suspicion cast upon them. The *White Swan* was not drifting, it was going full tilt—if sabotage had not been the goal, the small boat would have had time to veer away from the *Anabelle*, as the *Anabelle* was cruising gently, according to the cabin boy, her speed down to about five knots. It seemed a distinct possibility that the Hausmanns were aiming for the *Anabelle*. Target: Admiral Bailey.

The testimony of the tugboat master:

> *We were rounding a bend near Bowen Is-land, when the storm blew down from Squamish, suddenly; I had logs in tow and I made for a cove at Bowen, and left them—the waves were pretty high by that time, and the boats in question were covered by the island. We were making pretty slow time, even going full throttle, when we rounded the bend—it took us a good half hour to get there—with the heavy seas, we were afraid at one point we might take on too much water—the ship had already gone down. Our first thought was that it was just one boat—there was no sign of the other one. We were concerned for survi-vors, and we tried to draw near, but the storm was pretty fierce and we were still too far away; there was debris floating, deck chairs, boxes, but no sign of any people. The coast guard was still not in sight, and we circled the site, over and over—there was no one we could find.*
>
> Question: *Did you have any notion as to*

why the sinking happened so quickly?

Answer: *None that has not already been brought up. If it were an amidships collision, I'm sure enough damage could be done immediately.*

Did you have any suspicions about the motive of the White Swan?

I did not see the collision so I cannot say for sure. It seems very odd. Surely no one would head straight for another boat on purpose.

Unless they were bent upon the destruction of the other boat...

I don't know about that.

There was more information on the Hausmanns. A letter from the brother of Thomas Hausmann, protesting the charges; they—the Hausmanns—were of good family, owners of a dry goods shop, had been British subjects since the end of the last century. Both he and Thomas had served in the military. He is filled with grief at the deaths of his brother and sister-in-law and devastated by the charges levelled at them. His letter ends with news of persecution in London—simply because of his name, the shop had been vandalized, and he, himself, cut by a rock thrown through the window. He is sick at heart.

A query from the judge: *was there not a foreignness in the phrasing of the letter?*

The mother of Bess Hausmann, née Lawson, testifying to the goodness of her daughter's character, her domesticity, the cheerful letters home telling of her daughter's joys and difficulties in setting up a new home in the wilderness, with no civilization for miles. (If they lived outside Vancouver in 1915, Elizabeth thinks, they would be on the outskirts of a substantial city—scarcely a wilderness. How far away did they live? It is not clear.)

The mother is aghast that there would be any question of the Hausmanns being spies. They were patriotic to a fault.

A third letter is received from the mother of Thomas Hausmann. It is so stilted as to suggest (as does the prosecutor) that it is a translation from the German.

There is more testimony, most of it sounding more like testimonials. A eulogy to the late Admiral, his upright character, his unquestioned patriotism, and his endeavours to make the newly formed Royal Canadian Navy a true and vital arm of its parent, the Royal Navy. There was mention of his secret mission to Europe, rumoured to be of great importance to the cause of peace. He was much respected at the naval base in Esquimalt, and a memorial was held there which was attended by dignitaries from across Canada.

As for Ursula, she was international news, she was lauded for her courage, her beauty, her legacy to the theatre, the moving pictures. She was buried in New York in the vaults of the Cunningham family; her husband, it was reported, was too ill to attend.

The commission seemed to have been assembled hastily and seemed to reach a conclusion hastily.

Captain Farquarson's statement:

Though we cannot decisively state the reason for this tragedy, we are faced in this time of war with the possibility of an act perpetrated by traitors and instigated by the German War Office. More we cannot say.

He did not have to say more. The press had taken it from there.

∽

Elizabeth sitting in the stifling room thinks of the mockery of this trial. That these two ordinary people were guilty of such a crime, that they had become an infamous footnote to history.

Not that ordinary people did not do terrible things—the axe murderers, the men who raped, killed, dismembered women; their pictures in the papers usually showed bland, inconsequential faces. Rarely a tattooed member of Hell's

Angels with clotted hair and World War I German helmet.

But Elizabeth feels certain the Hausmanns were not spies. The facts needed to be stated. To let their bones rest. To grant them peace. To let them breathe.

She knows she is going off on a tangent, and that the Hausmanns are interfering with her story.

When she gets home from Victoria, she decides she will phone Paul Allenberg, the diver.

11

ELIZABETH IS SCARCELY BACK in her apartment when the phone rings.

It is her aunt Agnes. "I'm glad I got you," she says. "You're a hard one to find. And how are you then, Lizzie?"

Elizabeth sits on the couch, kicks her sandals off. "Just back from Victoria. How are you? I was thinking of phoning you."

"I know you're busy. Margaret, she says you're always busy. She says you came to see her, and you're dead skinny."

Elizabeth laughs. "She always thinks that. I'm OK."

"I was thinking of going over to Margaret's when I knew you were coming, but you know, that *Les*..." Her voice is thick with indignation. "Your mother knows I don't think much of him. The feeling is mutual, too, and that's for sure."

"I'll come and visit you. I haven't seen you for ages."

"Not for ages, and you know, I was going through these old pictures—I'll have to give them to you, Lizzie. Remember the picnic we had—oh, God knows when it was, you were a little thing—and we drove to some lake, and it turned out to be full of mosquitoes..."

"I remember—to Cultus Lake, you and Uncle Tony and

mother and father. I got bitten all over that day."

"And you went out too deep in the water, when your mum and me were putting out the lunch, and I thought your father would have a heart attack. He went out after you."

"I don't remember that." Why doesn't she?

"It was no big deal, except to him. You could swim. He was always so worried about you. Watching you like a hawk. He was some character, God rest his soul, full of all those stories…could sure always make me laugh, I'll tell you. Now Lizzie, you just come out. I'll sure be glad to see you."

She says she will. Next week.

She searches her mind for the swimming incident, but it has vanished completely.

She can't remember her father "watching her like a hawk."

It is a disturbing thought, which she quickly dismisses.

&

Elizabeth knew the *Anabelle* had been dived on shortly after the accident, in 1915; there were bodies still unaccounted for, though most had floated to the surface, many deposited on shore, on the mainland, on the little islands dotting the mouth of the inlet. The ships had sunk in deep water; the ocean bottom fell off sharply from the gentle green islands that surrounded it; few boats were ever brought up from its depth. The diving equipment of 1915 was primitive, the hard-hat-and-hose divers unable to stay down for very long and tethered to a ship. Bodies had been found in the *Anabelle*: Mrs. Jonathan Truro, the wife of the judge, pulled by the hair out of a cabin; Clarence Styron, the bank president, retrieved also from below decks. (From the same cabin, Elizabeth wonders?)

The bodies of the Hausmanns were found later.

The findings of the divers suggested the two ships had landed on the bottom at considerable distances from each other. The cabin boy thought he remembered the *Anabelle* going down by the prow—an impact on the delicate bow, its after-end long and slender sent skyward, could certainly cause it to split.

The small boat was never found.

The sensational sinking of the *Anabelle* was to be cast aside shortly by the darkening war news of 1915 as the Canadian Expeditionary Forces went into action, as the casualty lists became longer, and the barbarities of the Hun became increasingly brutal.

12

ELIZABETH IS ON THE DIVE BOAT. She is preparing to meet the *Anabelle*.

Elizabeth's buddy diver is Karen, a third year student in biology who works part-time at a dive shop. She is enthusiastic, pleasant, and regards the underwater world with a mixture of awe and romanticism. "Wait till you see the *Anabelle*," she says. "It's really crumbling away, but you can still see what it was like—beautiful. I found the bow first—which is smashed, it's in about sixty feet—the stern is in deeper water nearly a hundred feet down, and dark…it must have cracked in half over a ledge. When you think of the people in it, like your woman, the actress—it's like watching a movie. I also found part of the other boat—what was it—?"

"The *White Swan*" Elizabeth says. She is donning her rented suit, equipment.

"That's it—I think it *must* be, heavy keel, ribs…"

The dive master is Paul Allenberg, who has been diving with his wife, Patricia, for several years. In their suits, they look like figures from a medieval painting—long faces, both tall, hooded.

They have been briefing Elizabeth, who has never dived on this part of the coast.

"It's not like California," Paul says, "which can be sometimes boring—and certainly not like lakes which are inevitably boring. This is the best diving in the world. The most life, the most to see, and in these sheltered waters comparatively safe. Even the creatures down there are generally benign. You might see Old Grandfather—he's an octopus who's come out to watch us a couple of times. He likes divers. I would look out for wolf eel—they are usually friendly and tamable but they have sharp teeth."

He asks her where she learned to dive. "Ontario," she says. "Georgian Bay...I did both the certificates there—the open diving and deep diving. It's cold—freezing, most of the time."

"I've heard there's some wrecks there."

"I've seen what might have been a piece of one, hard to tell." She wasn't looking for wrecks. Not then.

The boat operator, Joe, who came here from Pittsburgh in 1968 as a conscientious objector—he is quite adamant that he was not a draft dodger—is an ocean man, who lives in it and on it. He is deeply tanned, bearded, wears a navy blue Greek fisherman's cap, and keeps a stack of science fiction comic books in his cabin.

The diver's flag is in position; because of the depth a descending line is being used. They are in their wet suits and putting on the cumbersome, awkward equipment which makes moving on land so difficult. Elizabeth pulls on her hood, gets Paul to help her slip on the tank. (They have checked diving time—fifteen minutes at the bottom—gone over buddy signals.) They add weight belts, masks, and finally fins, making them helpless, clown-footed, walking better backwards than forwards, so suited they cannot sustain themselves, must lean against bulkheads for support.

Elizabeth feels the tingle she has always felt as she enters the water.

The west coast ocean is indeed teeming with life.

Elizabeth is aware of floating down a wall, sees masses of

white anemones, sponges, rockfish, sea cucumbers the colours of the ocean—all colours, yellow and purple, orange and
pink. She has a sense of familiarity, as if she has been through
all this before; the ocean is a place of comfort, of safety,
everything benign and gentle. Dropping into this depth, the
confluence of colour, Elizabeth in her scuba gear feeling she
could fly forever through the rainbows, moves with the fish in
snakelike motions through rocks and ledges.

The Allenburgs have cautioned the divers: current, broken
fishing line, small boats. They carry knives against kelp, grass,
derelict lines.

Elizabeth knows the rules. She is enchanted by the ocean
bottom, a small fish stops for her, she reaches out tentatively,
strokes it, and turns to look at Karen as the fish wriggles in
appreciation like a cat.

Under the round coast mountains, under the friendly
placid ocean, danger seems remote.

The waters received her father. They did not kill him.

They have reached the *Anabelle*. Paul points and Elizabeth
swims slowly towards what at first looks like a mound of
barnacles, but the barnacles reveal themselves, turn into the
clear outline of a slender broken prow. The remains of the
Anabelle have been softened by kelp waving over them like
transparent shrouds.

Meeting the *Anabelle*, Elizabeth feels a sense of awe. This is
Ursula's ship. She glides along the fragmented, sloping deck,
following the line of the rail. The visibility is amazing; from
bits of rotting barnacled floor boards she notes the tentacles of
octopus, and thinks about how even foreign objects—dead
ships—are put to use in the economy of the sea. The wheelhouse has turned into kindling; there are copper-coloured
rockfish surrounding the kindling, lingcod and cloud sponges
rising in plumes of smoke. Elizabeth shivers in the cold, and
realizes that this much is left of the *Anabelle* because of the
searing chill of the sea at sixty feet down. The *Anabelle* has
settled into puddles of silt, which have cushioned the remains
and mummified them.

Elizabeth is suddenly overcome with the idea of Ursula, alive on her yacht, the testimony to her wealth. She reaches out to touch the rail with her gloved hand...she is stopped abruptly by her view of the *Anabelle* amidships, cracked in half. The ground is pocked with barnacle-covered objects—Elizabeth does not know if they are sea objects or invasive bits of the *Anabelle*.

Elizabeth has only begun her survey of the *Anabelle* but the others are moving off. Karen is pointing, and reluctantly Elizabeth follows. Paul and Patricia have already disappeared. She realizes she is descending, the sea floor falling off in an abrupt shelf, and that the waters are darkening. The Allenbergs in the lead are using their lights, and she reaches for hers; they are surrounded by blackness now. Karen is close beside her, Elizabeth is aware of her only as an outline, her light splashing like Elizabeth's on curious fish with large vacant eyes who stare at them as they descend, and suddenly they have reached bottom. The cold is intense; their lights play on the shadowy bulk of a huge rudder and the graceful lines of the *Anabelle*'s stern. The propeller has been long since removed, though Paul has said he found the end of its shaft. Elizabeth swims closer, her light trained on the deck—it is covered with thick mud. She is staring into the inner chambers of the wreck. Karen gives her a danger sign; Elizabeth knows wrecks can be precarious, but on her own, she would love to tunnel into the *Anabelle*, to look at the cabins, the salon. She draws back, however, and floats along the rail, noting the *Anabelle* is heeling to starboard, its midsection cut off, the wound bandaged by barnacles, sea whips. Paul points to a huge object, partially eaten with rust and festooned with long arms of kelp; she swims over to look, and realizes this must be the boiler of the *Anabelle*, at the same time notes something towering over her, leaning as if about to fall over, the steam engine covered with huge white barnacles and sea anemones, the upper portions of the cylinders holding waving arms of kelp. Seeing this decaying machinery, even more than the outline of the *Anabelle*, links the story for Elizabeth to reality.

She floats around the crushed stern, recognizes the cement ballast; there are splintered accretions, rounded objects strewn alongside the ship, as there were near the bow, objects that look intrusive, anchors for barnacles and sea weed.

Like we are intrusive, she thinks; it strikes her suddenly as absurd: long, unbelievable creatures, floating on our stomachs under the water, bubbles of air coming out of our mouths. Elizabeth is joined by a lingcod who swims close and stares with its great bulging eyes and then swims hurriedly away.

Karen is shivering; she holds her arms close to her body to signal and Paul Allenberg gives the up sign. Elizabeth shakes her head; she is freezing, but she is not ready to go. She signals up in the direction of the bow.

Paul has swum over, he is emphatically giving the up sign, and she and Karen ascend, Karen telling her to slow down, and Elizabeth slows, conscious of the price to pay for a quick ascent.

They hand their tanks to Joe, who helps them up—his grip is strong, and it is then that Elizabeth realizes the chill of the water—she is gripped in a spell of shaking, so violent it surprises her. Joe rushes into his cabin for hot coffee.

They take off their suits, don sweaters, and Joe throws a blanket around Elizabeth's knees. The hot coffee, the strength of the sun is restoring her.

"You stayed down too long, Elizabeth, come up when you get cold...it's not safe for you or your diving buddy," Paul tells her.

"It was OK," Karen says quickly, "but no longer than that...not even if you've dived a lot."

"I know—I got carried away. It was so marvellous seeing the *Anabelle*."

"You can literally get carried away." Patricia Allenberg is now a Modigliani figure in her shorts and hooded sweatshirt, elongated, spare. She is as serious as her husband. "We have to insist if people dive with us that they obey the rules. There are too many divers getting into trouble."

Elizabeth feels like a child being chastised. "Yes, sorry. I should have known better."

"It's quite an impressive wreck, don't you think?" Karen is stretching on the deck, lying back on her elbows.

"It's wonderful, the stern especially."

"Did you notice all the silt? That's what's preserving her—that and the cold."

"Everything's been picked off," Paul says, "the anchor, the name plate, the bell—things like that go..."

"Where is the *White Swan*?" Elizabeth asks.

"Oh, close by—we'll see it next time. At least I think that's what it is...it seems about the right size." Karen's face is round like a child's, her voice has a child's high excited timbre. "I don't think anyone's bothered much with it, no one seems to know too much about it...except you, Elizabeth, I think this whole thing is so exciting. We've found bottles—I mean, Paul and Patricia found most of them. I found two."

"What kind?"

"Lots of liquor bottles near the *Anabelle*, and two bottles of pickles that looked as if they were put up yesterday."

"What do you do with the things you find?"

"We take them to the Maritime Museum. There's been nothing really detailed done with this wreck. It's been so picked to pieces, so known about...in a way, it's sad."

Elizabeth also thinks it is very sad; she is now feeling the exhaustion of her activity in the cold water.

She has seen the *Anabelle*, and it has proved nothing. But of course, she is not sure what she is looking for.

13

ELIZABETH HAS SET UP SHOP in the apartment. Her portable computer, set on a table that faces the wall, looks away from the mountains and ocean.

Ursula is now stored among ten disks; I'm writing a series, Elizabeth thinks.

She has pinned up a reproduced photograph of Ursula on a bulletin board edged with kittens chasing fluffy balls—all the stationery store had available. Ursula stares in disdain at the cute kittens; she is dressed splendidly in a gleaming dress, a long train, holds a fan in her hand, looks like a Christmas ornament.

The phone rings. Elizabeth hastily exits the computer, and rushes to answer.

"Hello, is that Elizabeth...Elizabeth Morrison?"

"Yes."

"Oh, *hi*, it's Susan Mittleton...I'm in town."

"Susan...what are you doing here?"

"I'm giving a talk at the university..."

"Virginia Woolf."

"Of course. Actually, there's a conference. I'm only here

for a couple of days. How about lunch or something?"

"I'd love to. You say."

"OK, I'm talking just before lunch tomorrow...eleven till noon...I could see you just after. In the Buchanan Building, Room A90."

"I'll come to listen to you, Susan. Virginia Woolf and what...?"

"The Letters—the emerging consciousness...my pet project—you've heard it all before."

Elizabeth *had* heard it before, over endless cups of coffee in the staff lounge. "I'd like to hear you, anyway," she says.

"Don't feel obliged, Elizabeth."

"Oh, I don't. Looking for an excuse to escape Ursula for a little while."

"Who?"

"My woman. The biography."

"Oh, of course, how's it going?"

"Honestly, I don't know. I think other people are trying to get into the act."

"Others are writing about her?"

"No, no, I'm being obtuse, I think, Susan. I mean, I'm going off on tangents."

"Tell me about it...listen, I've got to go, I'm looking forward to seeing you tomorrow."

∽⌇

The room where Susan is to speak is an amphitheatre, half full, mainly women. Elizabeth takes a seat beside the aisle; Susan says "hi" on her way past. She is dressed as always in colours subtle to the point of extinction, a long skirt that looks as if it were made from a blanket. Yet Elizabeth knows Susan pays a good deal for her clothes.

At the podium she adjusts her wire-rimmed glasses, tucks

her long hair (centre-parted, the archetypal style of the seventies which Susan has never updated) behind her ears and clears her throat.

There is quiet that settles in ripples, slowly.

Susan is not an electric speaker; her voice is soft and without emphasis.

She talks of the letters of the young Virginia Stephen, the writer's care for what she is doing, the tough-minded exploration, dissection of emotions, her reaction to family deaths, to her marriage to Leonard Woolf, to her succeeding emotional breakdowns; "the earth seems swept very bare—and the amount of pain that accumulates for some one to feel grows every day."

Woolf's struggle for "a room of her own" touches Elizabeth, who thought at first she might fall asleep listening to Susan's soporific voice in the stuffy amphitheatre.

She had not slept well the night before. A crowd of hot-tubbers had been partying far into the night, so close they seemed almost outside her bedroom. At one point, Elizabeth had got up to look at them, annoyed and amused—naked bodies under a spotlight, three men and a woman in a tub.

Rub a dub dub.

It had seemed to Elizabeth that there was something absurd there, some comment on the age, but she was too exhausted to formulate it.

Susan's talk is greeted with enthusiastic applause. Elizabeth waits by the small platform while Susan fields comments, questions.

They lunch in the nearby Student Union Building, finding a table near the window. Over the fringe of trees, the ocean sprawls flat and luminescent, filled with sun spots that move like sequins. A waitress hastily clears up leftover watermelon rinds and coffee cups.

Susan chooses a vegetable salad, Elizabeth orders a hamburger. And doesn't enjoy it. She realizes she's being childishly defiant—she'd been preaching to Greg about cholesterol; she wants to break her own rules.

Elizabeth finds herself talking non-stop about Ursula, diving, Bess. She says apologetically, "I'm babbling. You must be bored stiff."

"Not at all, it's fascinating." There is a pause. The window pane is now filled with sun; Elizabeth pulls over the fibreglass curtain.

"And how are you—I mean *personally*? I've worried about you." Susan is speaking softly, her eyes filled with concern.

"I'm OK. Doing surprisingly well."

"You know, Elizabeth, I saw Greg in the supermarket. He looked awful. You haven't heard from him?"

"No. We decided not to get in touch. What do you mean— he looked awful?"

"Well, distracted, unhappy—you know."

"Did he?" Poor Greg, thinks Elizabeth. She wants to phone, immediately, and then realizes she mustn't.

"I shouldn't pry, I guess, but you must miss him." Susan speaks cautiously.

"You never pry, Susan." Elizabeth smiles at her. "I do miss him sometimes. The book is a godsend. I'm surviving."

"It must be nice to be back home. With family."

"It's odd. Difficult in a way. It raises a lot of old memories—spectres."

"Your father—of course, that must be difficult. Even after all these years. My mother's been dead—what is it—eleven years, and I still miss her, everything—my relationship with her seemed so *unfinished*. If you know what I mean."

"Yes." Elizabeth knows. "And how do you finish it? Are you even supposed to?"

"Yes, in some way. I believe that. There's always a vacuum, of course." Susan looks at her watch "Oh, damn, there's a talk I want to go to—Lillian Gerwith, from London. Know of her?"

"No."

"*The Female Voice*."

"Oh, yes, I heard about the book."

"Fascinating woman. Want to come?"

"I don't think so, thanks, Susan. I think I'll just have

another cup of coffee and sit and vegetate a bit. Call me before you go back."

Elizabeth finishes the dregs of the coffee, thinks about Susan's remarks, about the unfinished business, and feels a curious emotion welling up in her—an emotion which she finds hard to define. She cannot erase from her mind her aunt's words—her father watching her like a hawk—the image seems to her ominous. She had once seen a hawk, a small kestrel, grey with white markings and a Persian cat face, descend upon a wounded seagull. She had run down to the beach, watching in horror the doomed writhing of the gull fastened in the strong talons. She had felt a sense of desperate helplessness as she screamed, threw pebbles at the hawk who turned its beautiful face to her, uncomprehending, unmoving, secure in its innocence.

Hawks were predators.

Her father, watching her like a hawk.

Nothing seems clear any more. Even Susan, her friend, suddenly belongs to a world that is far away, has dwindled in importance. She is not of the coast.

Her students would say, "No problem, Dr. Morrison, it's all easy, our futures are quite clear. We can have it all." And it never occurred to them that they might run out of time and energy or tangle themselves up with their own pasts.

14

As Elizabeth got older there were the dates: initially forays to the Saturday matinees with squeaky boys growing out of their pants, wearing high-topped smelly running shoes; school dances, boys with sweaty hands staring in terror at the nuns posted like disapproving statues at various crucial intervals around the room; the boys growing into men who groped and begged; all of them ridiculed by her father. Elizabeth dressed by her mother in stiff dresses embroidered with ric-rac, trimmed with sequins, stuffed with petticoats, tall, so that she looked down on most of the junior high boys, with curly hair that frizzed into tendrils in the rain, brown eyes ("faun eyes," Greg had called them), and a skinny athletic body. She was good at sports, especially basketball which the private school girls played in old-fashioned-looking tap dance shorts. She felt unnatural in frills, like her grandmother's tall black telephone covered by a cellophane doll in a crinoline. She was happier in jeans and her dad's big plaid shirts.

She had a disdainful smile which she practised in front of the mirror.

Her father's laughter at the ineptitudes of all the boys

filling Elizabeth's mind. She had an occasional crush, but it was not lasting. The boys seen across a room through smoky music, in clusters at corners might be intriguing—up close they faded, metamorphosed into faint, uninteresting life forms. And floated off. If she felt a twinge of resentment that her father always found the boys, the young men, lacking, she had to admit he was right—they were inane and vacant.

15

ELIZABETH STARING AT THE SMALL television: the apartment is darkened, she has turned the lights low feeling the foreshadowing of another migraine headache, she has had the coffee, the Fiorinal and Gravol. She should not be staring at a flickering screen, but it is something to hold on to, some wavering piece of reality, a voice affirming she is here, will not float away.

It is "National Geographic": an underwater archaeologist is diving in a sink hole in upper Florida. The scene is surreal—middle-European tourists have crowded into the shallow section, corded off, soaking in the minerals, only their heads and shoulders visible; they wear enormous hats, they are singing in a strange language, pictures from ominous children's books, descended from Alice; they sway gently; they are separated from the archaeologists who plunge into the hourglass of the sink hole, broad at the top and bottom, curving in the centre to create a funnel.

The archaeologists are finding human remains, two hundred thousand years ago humans sat on the banks—then dry. They have left bits of their skull matter in the mineral waters, they were accompanied by creatures who resembled camels and sabre-toothed tigers.

The divers are descending one hundred and fifty feet; it is pitch dark, their lights shine on the bones, the minerals eat their regulators, they are gasping for air. They move backwards, through the ages.

Layer upon layer as they descend revealing a more primitive strata.

Through the funnel is the most difficult, squeezing down into the lowest reaches, where finally, the hole opens up, becomes wider, and everything is revealed.

Elizabeth feels the familiar throb on the right temple; the middle-Europeans rock and sing; the sink hole is curing them of all their aches.

The Florida condominiums edge closer.

This is primeval swamp; it may be filled by developers.

And the ancient past, the bones, buried, smothered.

Elizabeth feels the indignity; the picture is beginning to break up, the migraine aura is taking over. She wants those bones left alone.

She wants the divers, standing shoulders and heads visible now, their masks off, their regulators strapped on to their wrists now eaten, corroded, to be able to count the bones. To measure them.

She thinks the developer might have hired Greg for a feasibility study. Greg could deduce in precise charted language whether this project could be costworthy, whether the sink hole should be covered with buildings the colour of pink flamingos.

Elizabeth burns with more indignation. She needs coffee now, and a mouthful of food to ward off the pain that is coming.

16

SHE HAS CARVED OUT A ROUTE for herself. From the apartment to the library, from the library to the apartment, shopping excursions among the new stores that line the main street near the university.

Everything has changed from her student days. The world has become cuter. Everything is cute; people wear cute sayings on their T-shirts, cute boutiques advertise cute cuddly animals, cute designer wrapping paper, toilet rolls.

"I'm not cuter," she thinks. Her face reflected back to her in store windows, in mirrors, is sometimes startling—mouth pouching, new shadows and lines; she is glad for the glasses which mercifully hide her eyes. She determines to pick up some hair colouring, Tahiti Brown, to cover the flakes of white at the sides of her temples. She has been using Tahiti Brown for at least ten years. The intrusive grey, the lines—were they that apparent when she married Greg?

Certainly, the migraines were not.

Behind the stores that tinkle and smell strongly of floral bouquets (marketing research: pleasant smells attract customers), the stuccoed houses are glinting in the sun, their peaked roofs and upper stories mingling with the periscopes of apartments.

Everything used to be separate. Houses with their strong straight angles were divided into square rooms, did not angle to become family rooms, patios, entertainment centres, galleries like a maze in which each new turn reveals a new vista, but is still joined and therefore claustrophobic.

Her old house, the family house, a tall benign gargoyle looking over the inlet, a short walk to the water's edge, the front room, the dining room filled so often with Scots who brought celebrations with them. Filled the high ceilings with accordion music, whisky, reels and quadrilles, and Elizabeth watching them. Her dress fluffed out, white socks, patent shoes.

She is beside her father. She prefers to watch, has never learned the dancing skills to show off as her cousins—elegant Highlanders—have. "Lizzie is very like you." There is a pause in the quadrilles; her Auntie Jeannie's black crepe dress has a spreading stain under the arms; she has not been able to find her shoes. "Like as you can be, you two."

Her father winking at her.

Let it go. Let it all go. Not now, not when I'm trying to hang on. Hang on to the air hose that is connecting me to the world above…

∽

Over her head, a banner proclaims, "Lordy Lordy, Jimmy's Forty" and happy faces and balloons fly from the apartment window.

No crisp edge, all overlapping, celebrate and buy.

Elizabeth shuns the bok choy and jalapeno peppers and jimica and fills a shopping bag with lettuce, celery and carrots. I'm middle-aged, un-yuppie, and out of it, she thinks.

Or am I being too cynical? Greg had called her that once—more than once.

"Pain-in-the-ass know it all," she usually answered him back.

Greg was *au courant*, investigated the present with painstaking interest, rarely became indignant.

While I, Elizabeth thinks, have always been out of date. And then realized that even the expression is old-fashioned, something Will might say.

So be it, she thinks. Out of date, out of marriage, out of my element which has become the dry searing prairie plains, into this tangle of confusion.

She feels suddenly as if this place is deliberately harassing her. It is beautiful, so lush that it is almost embarrassing—like Christmas, everything brought out at once, overpowering, relentless.

17

THE FOLLOWING WEEKEND ELIZABETH looks for the *White Swan* without success.

Karen is the only one who has seen it; she says it was northwest of the *Anabelle*. She thinks. Because she hadn't checked her compass...

They consult their compasses, but find only more giant sponges, rockfish and enormous crabs who scuttle off at their coming, walking sideways, their shells brilliant orange. They notice comic faces that move towards them, teeth bared, bodies accumulating after them, like snakes. Paul gives the danger sign and Elizabeth realizes these are wolf eels who slither among the bull kelp, and she moves off quickly.

"That's so frustrating," Karen says—they are back on the dive boat. "I'm sure the *White Swan* isn't far away...the trouble is, I didn't think too much of it. It didn't seem important."

"It's quite recognizable, is it?" Elizabeth, stretching in the sun, is disappointed they haven't found the Hausmann's boat.

"Yes, it is—you can really tell what kind of a boat it was. I didn't know what it was at the time, but I knew it was an old ship—you can just tell—they're built differently. And I love looking at wrecks underwater..." Karen is bent over, towel-ling the front of her hair which had escaped from her hood. "We'll keep on looking...it sure couldn't have drifted away."

∽

Elizabeth and her father are walking beside the ocean, her father on the dirt path by the tracks, Elizabeth balancing on the rail, holding his hand. There are old pilings, like part of a drowned village, jutting up through the water. Her father says they are the remains of piers where ships docked many years ago. Where are the ships now? Elizabeth asks. Oh, long gone, her father says, fifty, sixty years. And the people? They would be very very old now, her father says, and Elizabeth looks at the pilings and thinks about the young sailors who docked at the piers and who grew older and sailed away. Thinks of the distance in time, and cannot measure it.

∽

Elizabeth has met Julia Matheson, a post-doctoral student in sociology—she'd met her at the Graduate Centre. Elizabeth was balancing her tray, looking for a seat in the crowded room.

Julia took her purse off a chair, and beckoned Elizabeth. "Here, take a seat—I was supposed to meet someone, but by now I know they're not coming."

Elizabeth finds Julia easy to talk to. They meet again for coffee, they tell each other the essentials.

"I'm interested," Julia says. She is understated in dress and in manner, hair short, fastened with a barrette like a composition doll of the thirties. She is altogether doll-like, tidy, her gestures small, closed.

Beside Julia, Elizabeth feels clumsy, enormous.

"I'm interested in your subject. Why did you choose her—the actress?"

"She's more than an actress; she was an entrepreneur...but I suppose you're right—she was more of an actress than anything. Her whole life was a grandiose act. That's why I like her—she's fascinating."

Julia is cutting up a muffin into small, precise pieces. "She made herself up?"

"That's it." Elizabeth is eating carrot cake which is excessively sweet and crumbly. "She did what she wanted to do."

"Do you think so?"

"Yes. Absolutely. Given the constraints of the society in the early 1900s—she was working within the framework."

"She used men, you mean? That's what women often had to do."

"Yes, they did. But she took off from that point...eventually became more powerful than the men around her."

Julia nodded. Her gaze was direct, she seemed unhurried and truly interested, though Elizabeth felt there was some challenge being given to her.

"You're at U.C.L.A.? Are you an American?"

"No. Actually, I'm a Canadian...down-easter...P.E.I."

"Really? I'm native west coast, transplanted to Calgary."

"Beautiful country."

"Too cold. Too bright. I miss the clouds and rain."

Julia laughed. "And everyone who comes out here misses the sun and snow. Did you grow up in the city?"

"No, outside the city. Cedarglen—it's a suburb now, it was separate when I grew up, quite beautiful view of the inlet and mountains, but close to the city."

"Sounds lovely."

Outside the city. Elizabeth thinks of Tom and Bess Hausmann who lived outside the city. She senses Julia looking at her.

"Oh, sorry—I was woolgathering. I go off like this all the time. I was thinking about the other boat."

"The one that hit the *Anabelle*?"

"I've been looking at the transcripts. It was a time of great hysteria; no one questioned that the Hausmanns, the boat occupants, were spies..."

"You question it?"

"I absolutely do. Still, research gets you off in odd directions."

Elizabeth finishes her tea (coffee is starting to taste bitter to her). Before they leave each other, Julia and Elizabeth plan to meet at the Cultural Centre to see Mary Davenport (whom Julia had seen in Los Angeles) as Emily Dickinson.

That night, Elizabeth reads a review lauding the one-woman show, and Mary Davenport's complete transformation into Emily Dickinson and "her ability to project Dickinson's austere life."

As Elizabeth recalled from second-year English, there wasn't too much in Dickinson's world—an old house, old memories, a love affair which couldn't be consummated.

A woman in white disappearing down vast corridors, who spoke out of the Victorian hymnal in crisp, startling poems full of irony and vitality.

∽

The lobby is crowded before the opening. Elizabeth and Julia stand in line for a glass of wine.

"Are you here for the whole summer?" Elizabeth asks.

"Yes, pretty well." Julia is wearing a blue cotton jacket and skirt; under the jacket, a white blouse with Peter Pan collar. She has no jewelry except for a silver band on her right hand.

"I'm actually lucky to be getting this much time to myself. I wasn't sure if the order would agree to it, but they did."

"The order? You're a *nun*?"

"Yes. Sorry, I thought you knew. I don't always bring it up."

"It's funny, Julia," (they were standing under a large fig tree which was spiralling its way towards a skylight) "because..." She paused.

"You mean, I remind you of nuns you saw or met or knew."

"Yes."

"It probably stays with you forever. I joined in the old days of the habit, and the strict formation when everything was measured. The discipline of the eyes—I remember that, the inward look away from temptation—seems far away now. All that emphasis on form...where did you go to school?"

"An academy, in Cedarglen actually. Very proper Nova Scotian nuns. Beautiful campus. I remember the campus with great pleasure."

(Even if I don't remember everything. If I sit in church now and want everything to be different.)

Mary Davenport is brilliant. In front of a bare curtain, in a theatre which had once been a church, which still contained a choir loft and seemed so church-like Elizabeth felt she could still smell candle smoke, Mary Davenport became Emily Dickinson. With limited movements of the body, the arms, she suggested the contained explosion that was Dickinson, the letters, the raging inner life held in check, in the spare figure in virginal white, her hair parted in the middle, a cameo culled from a proper Victorian milieu, her love for the married clergyman which could not be acted upon:

> I cannot live with You
> It would be Life—
> And Life is over there—
> Behind the Shelf
>
> The Sexton keeps the key to,

At intermission Elizabeth and Julia join the line to the washroom. Elizabeth says to Julia, "An intermission is often a time of suspense, what will happen in the next act. We know what happens here—in a sense, nothing."

"And yet everything," Julia says.

"She must have driven biographers crazy; I'd heard they'd resorted to making up material."

"There's much made of the frustrated spinster theme. Freudian stuff," Julia rolls her eyes. "I read a terrible biography. Written by a man, of course."

"As a nun, aren't you ever bothered by church structure? If there ever was a patriarchy..."

"Of course. But it's not much different from society in general. How equal are wives, for instance? Underneath the rhetoric who has the power? How many women heads of corporations are there?"

"Or full professors."

"Exactly. Things are changing, but not fast enough. There's a pool of talented, educated women in the Church. It would be a natural transition to a female clergy."

"Certainly many of the nuns who taught me were strong women."

"Of course. This male thing—the insistence that there can be no women priests because Christ was male, and the apostles were male—nonsense. There were all kinds of women in the early Church who seemed to have shared responsibility with men. In fact, did you know they've found a fresco in the catacombs that shows a depiction of the Last Supper in which there are many more than twelve present, and in fact, many of those present are women. When the early Christians retreated to the caves, there were women who conducted services...Don't get me started...it's my pet hobby horse..."

In the second part of the performance, Elizabeth listens, and watches Mary Davenport, and thinks about Dickinson's life.

As freezing persons recollect
The snow—
First chill, then stupor, then
The letting go.

If she had married the clergyman, would there have been any poetry?

18

ELIZABETH'S MARRIAGE HAD TURNED rapidly from poetry to prose. She was no longer alone in her apartment, eating her microwaved meals, writing when she wanted to, sometimes even in the middle of the night, in a sweatsuit and bare feet, addled with instant coffee. Suddenly she was structured, circumscribed. There was somebody else wanting something, taking something away. Time became an enemy, the day, the night divided into regular hours

But she had bought into it. The old myth. Gladly. Contrary to all the learned and accumulated wisdom of feminism, she wanted to be a wife. She took her husband's name, determined that she would learn how to cook—one of her first acts as Mrs. Greg Andrews was to buy an apron that said "A-1 Cook", and Julia Child's *The French Chef* (she would not be a meat-and-potatoes cook like her mother) to create gourmet meals—and to that end she took a brief night school course. For Greg, who was exceedingly neat, she tried to pick up her belongings; she was used to dropping things, accumulating clothes on chairs, leaving dishes in the sink. She marvelled at Greg's ability to slot and differentiate: time, articles, his wallet at night in a special box, keys hung from the mouth of a pink wooden poodle he'd bought at a garage sale. And which she'd objected to.

He didn't really care about the cooking. He wasn't demanding it. "I can cook for myself," he said one night when she took a burned Beef Bourguignonne out of the oven, putting the dish down with a screech. "Look, Lizzie, you do your own work."

"But then, you'd only eat grease, fry stuff. You can't cook." She was on the brink of tears.

(Her mother's voice: You're thin as a stick, Greg.)

"So what, who cares? I survived so far."

"You'll die of high cholesterol."

She scarcely recognized herself—who was this person who spoke through her, this medium, the spirit of dead wives, trapped and powerless?

Greg, holding her: "Come on, Lizzie, you don't need to pamper me." He was tall, powerful, he played tennis and squash, his grip on her was strong.

The words automatic: "But I want to do things for you."

But she didn't. Why was she saying those things?

∾৻ঌ

Ursula nagged at her. Even through the ordeal of the baby that never was, that ended up in a miscarriage, filling Elizabeth with mingled despair and relief. Greg had wanted a baby more than Elizabeth did, he and his first wife—who died of breast cancer—had produced no children. He was naturally good with children, held dialogues with them that Elizabeth could not follow. Tender, uncomfortable dialogues.

Ursula visited her in the hospital, urging her to get on with the work. Elizabeth developed an infection after the miscarriage, her temperature had soared into hallucinations, Greg had stayed beside her. When she came out of her stupor she saw him, his face deep with concern, unshaven, in a sweatshirt dotted with grease. She felt grateful to him, apologetic.

Her mother had flown out from the coast, though she hated planes. Her face was funereal and solemn. "It's the will of God," she said, "the longer you put off having children, the harder it is—there's not so much chance after forty." She had taken Elizabeth's hand and held it gently; Elizabeth had seen her mother holding the hand this way of her dying grandmother, of an uncle. I'm not terminally ill, Mother, she thought. She also wanted to say that she hadn't put it off—it was never intended. Instead she started to cry. She had been emptied out. The baby had deserted her. She seemed to be crying all the time. The counsellor who told her she didn't release her feelings enough didn't know what she was talking about.

Later when Elizabeth thought about it, she realized she might have loved the baby out of all proportion.

"I know what you're going through," her mother said, "I had two miscarriages." Elizabeth was startled.

"I didn't know that."

"No, no one knew."

"Dad must have..."

"Well, yes, of course...I think it would have been nice to have had more children." A child for *you*, Elizabeth thought—the idea of a brother or sister, someone else in the family, struck Elizabeth as odd and inappropriate.

"Spoiled brat!" Greg had yelled at her once when she slammed a door in his face. "Daddy's little girl...no wonder you can't love anyone."

"What about you?" she yelled back at him. "You're still in love with your first wife..."

There had been a moment's quiet. "That's a rotten thing to say, Lizzie." Greg's voice hurt, indignant.

"What you said was rotten, too."

They had come to that. Raising up ghosts to throw into each other's faces.

Let it go.

∾

Elizabeth at University: enjoying her English course; she was reading *The Waste Land, The Four Quartets*—she was dazzled by Eliot's imagery, the phrases that rushed out at her (she ignored, as she always did, the technical discussions, the placement in a larger framework). She took the words and applied them to history, her own history. Realizing she was part of a continuum. Time before and after. Scarcely now. Her people who had lived on their rocky island, and their people before them, and all the bones that made the paths they took, and the drowned sailors.

She began to see it all. Her grandmother's photographs, people pausing for the camera in their rumpled clothes, with sober, bemused expressions or artificial smiles, pausing only long enough from the fishing, the gutting, the digging of peat to document their own records, to marry, to come of age, to be confirmed.

She wanted to talk about these things. And about the sketches in the ancient newspapers in the library, and how the sketches turned into photographs, so that what had been heroic in outline revealed itself to be only blood and terror. Dead men and dead horses. And the people who killed each other, who got up and carried on, repeating themselves forever. She became captivated by history, saw it as a line that undulated like thick waves in the sea.

19

ELIZABETH IS AT THE MICROFICHE. She is reading letters to the editor in the Vancouver *Province*, November 1915, denouncing the Germans who reside in Canada.

Will hands her a letter. "Thinking of the Hausmanns rang a bell. I dug up this letter—never sent, it would appear—from Bess Hausmann, the wife."

Elizabeth looks up. "Where did it come from?"

"Again, who knows? It was in an envelope entitled, 'The *Anabelle*,' but in a box full of the 'Proceedings of the Imperial Order Daughters of the Empire'..." Will grins at her; he smells of smoke—he says he's down to ten a day.

The letter is addressed to Mrs. D. Lawson, Hollies, Windsor, England; there is no stamp—it is the same precise, tiny hand of the writer of the account book. It is redolent of west coast, mould, dead leaves; Elizabeth fancies she smells smoke, possibly a hint of ocean. It is dated October 2, 1915 (only a few weeks, Elizabeth thinks, before the sinking).

> *Dear Mother,*
> *At last, Tom's boat is finished; and the*

White Swan *(Tom insists on the name — I think it sounds like an East End pub) is ready to be launched. I can't tell you how relieved I am. I have never known him to spend so much time on a project. Though he has sometimes fumed and cursed at the* White Swan*'s non-cooperation, he has never given up on her.*

He is so happy and I am happy for him. When you think he came out with his army pension, a small family stipend and how ill he was — you would not recognize the robust, tanned, laughing man he is now. I know now our move was for the best. Although after three years, after the building of our home, I still miss London so much, and you and my dear sisters and brothers. There are times when I weep still with homesickness.

There are other times, like today. The sun is shining. There was a full harvest moon last night.We are still collecting rosemary, thyme, sage from the garden, as well as spinach, cabbage, cauliflower, even tomatoes. I will take off the last tomatoes today.

Can you picture your pampered city daughter a happy gardener? By the way, thank you again — I am always thanking you — for the parcel. The gardening gloves are wonderful, so thick, and the face and hand balm exactly what I need.

There is simply not the quality here at our local store, which is in itself a long, long walk. And to go into Vancouver of course is a day's journey by foot and then via streetcar.

And even then, as Aunty Peggy noted when she visited, the goods tend to be shoddy. There is simply not the care taken. People are very indifferent and unreliable. I dislike this attitude — I found it in the girls I hired to help about the house—quite impudent, and lazy. Not at all like home.

And yet, Mother, when I write "home" I find I am conscious that England is not really home any more. We have made a new life for ourselves, and I think it will be some time before—if ever— we go to our old home.

As for the boat, it is quite handsome, and so it should be—three years of work; God help the person who says anything against the White Swan.

I must close. It is nearing dinner time, and I have a wonderful pot roast in the oven, with our own(!!) potatoes. Knowing how fussy Tom is about his food, you must congratulate me on learning how to cook, and indeed, becoming a good cook. Much better than the woman—a Mrs. Rabbitt!!—who came briefly to try her hand at cooking. Tom hated her food, all watery stews and vegetables so overcooked they were lifeless. He insists now that I do the cooking.

Again thank you for the parcel and your wonderful letters. If you could ship me a reliable and polite girl who is interested in working in a beautiful country, with a view of the ocean, and air that is sweet and clean, send her along. She must enjoy washing up, sweeping, drawing baths and working hard—I work now from sun up to sun down. Tom is never inside during the day.

You asked me too do I long for the old, comfortable days? Sometimes, but my heart is quite full. Quite content.

There is only one shadow. That business at home.

We see pictures of the soldiers drilling at

Hastings Park, the war fills the newspapers.

Tom says the White Swan *might be used for some sort of service.*

I think it is all wishful thinking. He and George Blackwell, our neighbour, like to talk about deeds of derring-do.

Tom, though healthier, is not up to his own dreams.

With all my love, and to Father, Alice, Lucy; say hello to Arthur and John.

Your daughter,
Bess

Elizabeth folds the letter carefully. Her hands are shaking; they often tremble now—she thinks it must be the migraine medicine. She takes the letter to Will; he is talking to a student helper, an earnest-looking boy with enormous spectacles. Elizabeth waits impatiently.

"Sorry," Will says.

"Have you read the letter?"

"Yes, I have—interesting."

"It certainly is; there's a lot about the *White Swan*, the boat—they're preparing to launch it. There's also 'this business in England'...I don't suppose you have any idea..."

"None at all."

"Bess sounds like a snob, and a doormat for her husband, but not like a spy."

"And what do you think a spy sounds like?" Will is smiling at her, and she realizes her words have come out all in a rush.

"I know what you mean, but it doesn't make sense..."

"I agree with you. The whole episode, the accusation, sounds quite fishy."

"Could you copy the letter for me?"

Will comes back with the copy. "How about a cup of coffee? Exorcising ghosts is chilling work I should think."

✑

That night Elizabeth dreams, but not of Greg. Her mother is dressed in a gown that ends just above her ankles—a dark dress, nun-like, the kind Julia might once have worn; her hair is piled up into a neat bun, but there are two curls at the side; the dress has no soft lines, it is stiff as if it were cut out of paper, like the cutouts that Elizabeth played with and kept in paper bags in a small cedar chest—she did not like dolls, preferring cutouts which you could toss out if you were tired of them.

Elizabeth knows in her dream—which wavers, making her feel queasy—that her mother's form is stiff because she is wearing a corset under the drab dress with its long white apron. Elizabeth's mother becomes her grandmother who always wore a corset, old and ravaged with arthritis, she sat upright in her corset, listening to the radio.

The woman in the long dress is looking out the window, has her mother's face again; there is a man getting into a boat. She looks at him tenderly; there is soup bubbling on the stove, a large black and silver wood stove, her grandmother's stove, but the man in the boat is not her grandfather, who was round and pleasant and lost in a world of his own devices.

The man is young. And suddenly Elizabeth in her dream realizes her mother never wore corsets or a long stiff dress or such an enveloping apron.

And she realizes she is watching Bess Hausmann, the devoted wife, who died with her husband. The boat sets off; Elizabeth feels more and more queasy and wakes with the beginning of another migraine headache.

She switches on the bedside light, reaches for her medicine.

She plumps the two pillows behind her and sits up, feeling sicker and sicker. She wishes the bed was straight; its roundness seems to accentuate her feeling of unreality. The aura might or might not come—the waving lines, the sun spots on the walls when everything breaks up into flashing lights, contracting and expanding.

Only a person with migraines could have written *Alice in Wonderland*, she thinks.

She puts down her unease over her dream to the headache, when everything becomes ominous, the routines of everyday life part of a horror movie.

Julia had told her of a nun, a friend of hers, who had had to leave the order because of blinding migraines. "That was in the old days," Julia said, "when there were more rules—she told me she felt suffocated." The ex-nun was now married, running a bookstore, and headacheless.

"Have you ever thought about leaving?" Elizabeth had asked.

"Very seriously. But it's OK—I believe in what I'm doing, in spite of things I want to see changed. And maybe staying in can change things more rapidly. Besides, I seem to do better within this kind of framework."

Elizabeth, at the time, had wondered what kind of framework *her* life fitted into.

She is conscious of traffic noises, of the city shifting with movement and sound, easing slowly into life. In her migraine misery, she thinks, I am trapped by the dead.

Ursula, Bess, her father: she wishes at this moment she had not come to the coast—she has left her husband and run headlong into her father.

She feels the indignity of her situation, but then everything here—in this beautiful place—is filling her with indignation.

Knowing she will not sleep for a while, she flicks on the radio, and there is only yuppie light rock on every station, with the exception of a religious channel which has a smooth-voiced commentator tackling the problems of looking after your money in a Biblically correct way.

Then there is a conversation between an editor for a religious magazine and the announcer regarding the great problem of homosexuals in the media.

And New Age Satanists.

The world is ready to be taken over by dark forces. Elizabeth thinks how important it is for people to hate.

The Satanists of 1915 were the Germans, the Huns. People who had gone to school in Germany could be ostracized. The collective hate of Vancouverites had been focused, if briefly, on the Hausmanns. Elizabeth starts to get sleepy; the nausea is subsiding, the headache only a vague ache on the left side of her temple. In the semiconscious state between waking and sleeping, she thinks—or dreams—about Bess Hausmann again, who is in Elizabeth's childhood home overlooking the inlet. She is standing on the porch above the steep steps, looking over the railing at the sinuous lines of the ocean, the upheaval of mountains...and although Bess is perfectly still, there is something sinister about the scene.

Then Elizabeth disappears into a dreamless sleep.

20

HER GRANDMOTHER'S DEATH. Her father, head bent, tears falling down his cheeks. Elizabeth was six. It was November; the leaves were nearly off the trees, dark, bleak. Her grandmother, a rouged mannequin laid out in a box quilted inside like her mother's sewing box, then the box sealed and her grandmother tucked away in the wet black earth, a piper in his sombre green and blue kilt sent slow, mournful notes into the slate sky.

She could think of that—it was removed, far away.

She could not remember her father's funeral.

The counsellor had looked at her, alarmed, when she mentioned that.

"Not at all?" she said.

Hardly at all. Only that it had been a sunny day; she remembered sun, but the pictures of that day were like snapshots shot into the light—fuzzy, spots and haloes, slow movements that were not part of discernible actions.

"Elizabeth," said the counsellor, "you have never grieved. You have never admitted this into your subconsciousness."

She was wrong. Elizabeth had never stopped grieving.

21

THE FOLLOWING NIGHT IN a dream Elizabeth meets Bess
Hausmann. It is a diving dream and it is quite clear, perfect.
She has heard of things like this: divers reporting visions of
lost sailors, drowned children, mermaids, seal people. The
seal people and mermaids were part of the mythology of her
Scottish ancestry; they were as real as the invisible funeral
processions that walked through houses, the dancing lights on
the water—as a child, she had believed all this as implicitly as
she had believed in her religion. If there were guardian angels,
and devils, and floating saints, it was no leap of faith to believe
in the turbulent spirit world of the Scottish Islands.

In her adult life she put aside some of these things.

But there is no question that the woman who floats towards her is Bess Hausmann. She is wearing a long coat, a
duster, over a grey dress—or is it grey?—the ocean has churned
up silt—belted at the middle. She is dressed as if she might be
ready for an automobile drive in an open dusty car. On her
head, a veil, tied under her neck.

She is floating towards Elizabeth; they are close to each
other and Bess stares at Elizabeth, a look curious and fright-

ened. Elizabeth wonders if Bess' fear might centre on the creature in the sleek suit, the hood and goggles, the tank.

The divers of 1915 had clumsy large space helmets, stood upright, and were tethered to their dive boats; they did not resemble slithering fish.

She seems then, from her expression, to have decided Elizabeth means no harm, and she stops, briefly, and smiles, a smile that is tentative and does nothing to erase the sadness in her eyes.

And as suddenly she ascends, floating upward without seeming to move. Elizabeth could never say that Bess had vanished, not as spirits do; she had drifted off, up through the ocean, Mary's assumption into heaven. Elizabeth wakes up, her mind full of white dots, things left out...a nagging sense that Bess is intruding on her book.

⧼⧽

Elizabeth underwater on the prairies.

The closest lake thirty miles outside Calgary, sinking silt and mud, and the four of them, Greg and Elizabeth, and a couple who worked in Greg's office—he an engineer, like Greg, she a draughts*person* (she underlines the *person*), walking like space aliens in their bizarre heavy equipment— heading into disappointing waters where salt and pepper granules float around waving grass, foggy, unrevealing water—whatever was down here kept to itself.

Elizabeth felt no interest in the couple. They conversed with Greg, not her, their plans more akin to Greg's, not hers. They were excited about the condo they'd just moved into, they had planned their lives, dividing them into neat five-year sections—in five years when the mortgage was down, she would have a baby—she would spend three months at home with the baby, and then she would return to work on a part-time basis. The milestones were lined up like dominoes to be knocked over: the baby, the summer cottage, the cruises, the move eventually to the coast.

It was the woman, Kelly, who volunteered all this information, but her husband—or was it her husband? Elizabeth never knew—made approving noises from time to time.

What Elizabeth remembers from that dismal outing is Greg's face as he looked at Elizabeth, the urgent expression— see how everyone's getting on with things—what's wrong with us?

Elizabeth had made plans—writing, teaching, the climb up the academic ladder...those were plans for herself—she was having difficulty with plans for *them*. Turning *me* into *us*. What was happening to her seemed as unclear as the lake bottom, shifting, changing. She found herself sometimes demanding, sometimes despondent, she was unrecognizable.

"I'm not making you happy..." Gentle Greg, his face full of self-pity.

"Why should you make me happy? That's so damn paternal..."

"Why can't we talk this out? I can't get anywhere with you." Greg again, pushing this time.

"Tough. Just leave me alone."

I feel, she thought, like a hostage being kept by a kindly terrorist—solicitous and caring, but watchful.

She was living in a surrealistic painting—Greg's eyes watching her, trying to divine her moods, and then his eyes multiplying so that in every room he was staring at her.

She sometimes wondered if, during her days with Greg, she had been quite right in the head. Her reactions were unfocused, confused; it was as if she had come up too quickly from a dive, with the bends, or brain embolism...she was restless, disagreeable, became addicted to aches and pains, the onset of migraine headaches...

And yet, through her misery, in the hallucinatory throes of the headaches, she sometimes felt that Greg—kind, managing, needy Greg—had not found himself a proper wife.

❧

Elizabeth underwater in the Bahamas.

Before Greg, a memorable dive. Elizabeth on vacation, finishing her Ph.D., leaving the bleak chill of grey Toronto for the bright pastels of the Islands—washes of pale colours that produced upon them more vibrant hues—blood red and ochre yellow, deep purple flowers and people all filling the air with a vibrancy she had never seen before.

Not the tourists—they put on holidays obviously and awkwardly with the new shorts and shirts—but the inhabitants, their laughter articulate, their movements unstudied. They moved among the flowers as naturally as gardeners in a vast limitless greenhouse.

She was travelling with her friend, Rhonda, who like Elizabeth had a teaching assistantship. It was Christmas break; Elizabeth wasn't going home to her mother's (over much protestations)—she was spending Christmas in the sun.

Rhonda, in her mid-thirties, was newly come back to school, was relishing her freedom.

"This is something I've dreamed of, Elizabeth." They were lying on the sand, their bodies covered with sun tan oil, both in minuscule bikinis, Elizabeth at twenty-seven becoming aware of a sag in her middle, and promising herself to stand up straight. "All the time I was married, I made Christmas dinner for my husband and his family and my family. Christmas to me meant a sea of exhaustion and confusion."

"I've always been home...my mother wasn't keen on me being away."

"You're the only child?"

"Yes."

"That makes it hard. Is your father alive?"

"No. That makes it different. If my father were alive I'd be home."

And we'd find a tree, she thinks, the mountains etched in

the acid clear December day, there would be few presents, many relatives. If it rained on Christmas day, she didn't remember, she never noticed, the weather moved inside, everything became gleeful.

Would she never stop this—living backwards? The counsellor had warned, "If you live too much in the past, you choke off the present."

The past was now tangled around her like an octopus and she was in its lair, which was round and curved and coffin-like.

Greg and Elizabeth fighting over Christmas: should they go to his parents, hobby farmers, strict, temperate, living frugally on a small expanse of farmland under the brow of the Rockies. In the clapboard house, the same sense of intrusion she felt with Greg—his parents, though pleasant and hospitable, were coiled like traps ready to spring shut.

They lived on information gathered from the television, newspapers, radio, saw life as a list of war casualties, information freighted with doom. Mostly they drew information from people, decoding it until it fit their interpretation of life.

"And your father—you must think of him at this time of year?" His wan mother by the wan Christmas tree.

(Your poor drowned father…how did it happen exactly?…)

What day. What year.

What time.

What time.

Strangulation:

Strangulation can be caused by the accidental inhalation of some foreign material. This obstructs the breathing, and is the most frequent cause of strangulation during a dive. Artificial respiration should be used and one should seek any obstruction and remove it.

22

SHE WAS THIRTY-NINE, AND SO WAS HE; she should have known he would carry his first wife into a new marriage. Not that he ever made comparisons—but Elizabeth knew she did not measure up to poor dead Marcia, who did not fumble at casseroles, who could wash without producing tie-dyed clothes, who was tender in bed, whose only fault was that she died of breast cancer. These were things Elizabeth knew from certain glints in Greg's eyes, from what he did not say, but which she divined from him. She was standing beside a dead woman who followed her around, admonished her.

It had all happened quickly. She was at a faculty Christmas party at Richard Baxter's, then her department head. It was quite usual, the food catered, set out perfectly on the Georgian table, in the small dining room with the Morris-patterned wallpaper, presided over by Richard's wife, who was getting drunker as the evening progressed and quoting some of Blake's more obscure poetry (her thesis specialty) defiantly, her face filled with spite when she looked at Richard. The department lech, who ran several consulting companies on the side ("Assertiveness Training for Profit and Mobility";

"The Effective Use of Time"), who was moving in on a voluptuous graduate student. A visiting professor who came from New York and was in a discipline called "Historical Literary Data Analysis Systems" was trying to collar people. He toiled at the computer endlessly and long lists of numbers which looked as if they should be in Greg's office spewed out of the printer—he was toothy, genial and effusive, trapping people in his office to chat because he missed "communicating," as he put it. He told Elizabeth he found Canadians reticent, puzzling. Elizabeth retreated when she saw him coming. The night she met Greg she had not been able to escape; she was perched on the edge of a chair, listening to Eliot rhapsodize on New York at Christmas. Greg had come with the History Department secretary, a bleakly inefficient and unsmiling young woman, who taught aerobics at a glittering health club and who spent a good deal of time at her desk doing word search puzzles, her sad dark-rimmed eyes looking accusingly at anyone who brought her work.

Elizabeth liked Greg immediately, liked the way he brought her a drink (the secretary had taken up with the lech). She was delighted when he gave her his more comfortable chair, asked her about her teaching, writing. He was an engineer working in a downtown office; he seemed to her refreshingly real in a roomful of unreality. Someone had brought a video cassette of sixteenth-century madrigal singing performed by the professor of renaissance studies and his coterie of fellow Brits on a local Calgary TV station. They were singing in Latin, they were wearing cowboy hats, and what endeared Greg to Elizabeth almost more than anything was the fact that, as the "Calgary Choristers" proceeded with their songs—their lutes playing, faces rhapsodic under their ten-gallon hats—she and Greg had exchanged glances, both of them suppressing laughter. But there was more in the glance—they were together, clearly, in a way that Elizabeth would have dismissed as hopelessly romantic. Elizabeth heady with wine and new love could have burst out singing "Some Enchanted Evening."

The time was exactly right.

She had just talked to her mother on the phone that afternoon. Her mother had said a cousin was arriving in town, would Elizabeth meet her, take her out (only if she had time, of course), there was a report on another cousin's new baby, the palatial mansion (in her mother's description) a nephew and his wife had just purchased.

Elizabeth had been dating a classics instructor whose apartment was literally a den of smoke and mirrors, reflections of the two of them everywhere, the air full of incense and candle smoke; he enjoyed watching himself: he was genial and careless, he stood her up twice—the last time he left her alone in Banff while he came home with another woman. She had told him off vociferously, and then, alone, cried with frustration and anger.

He was the last in a series of bad relationships.

Greg was different. She had not felt Greg to be possible. She was sixteen again, playing love songs on the radio, writing in her diary—they had gone back in time. Within two weeks they knew they wanted to marry.

Her first act was to phone her mother. To announce the marriage.

Her mother's surprise and consternation: it was so helter-skelter, so fast, was she sure? Yes, she was sure; Greg and Elizabeth together, a surge of desire, tenderness, their bodies breaking through the barriers to submerge in another atmosphere, twisted together, legs entangled, wet with lovemaking, Greg nibbling gently on her ear, her sense of being carried joyfully on the surface.

But it wasn't her he was holding, it was dead Marcia, disfigured, incomplete, who had eluded him.

❧

Nitrogen Narcosis, rapture of the deep, is one of the most dangerous enemies, because it is a friendly feeling, devoid of fear.

❧

On the holiday in the Bahamas, Elizabeth and Rhonda had dived on their first wreck.

They had come down on a student excursion, flying on the red-eye flight, lodging in an unfashionable and barren hut which must have been fifty years old, paper-thin, on a cliff— it didn't matter; the splendour of the exquisite coral sea and shore stood out against the new posh Travelodge on the beach below them.

They joined an excursion boat of divers heading for the wreck of the British mail boat, the *Pauline*. The ship had gone down close to shore in the 1840s and was a diver tourist stop, safe and yet spectacular, its deck collapsed to the bottom, steel beams encrusted with coral forming bulging archways. Elizabeth enjoyed the sensation of diving in warm seas; her dives so far had been in the chill of Lake Ontario and Georgian Bay. A wet suit hardly seemed necessary but was required of tourist divers. Elizabeth in her rented suit and mask slipped through the arches, wishing she could interpret the debris on the ocean floor—rocks in twisted shapes might well be pottery, although she was to learn that everything had long since been taken up.

She had worried about the dive to the wreck. How would she feel at her first sight of a dead ship? But the massive coral supports, the magnitude of the rotting deck filtered through the crystal water, had delighted her, filled her with exhilaration. She found herself annoyed when the expedition leader gave the sign to ascend.

She had not finished with this wreck.

Later Elizabeth tried to reconstruct the wreck in her mind, pull together the shifting coral, meld it like a jigsaw puzzle, but she found she could not put it together. Looking at the picture of the ship with its sails buttressed by steam, standing obediently at its Southhampton dock, she saw no relation to the wavering pieces under the sea.

Greg could do that. He had that kind of mind. The kind that put things together.

∽

The doctor on her migraines: they could be hereditary—did her parents have migraines? Not her mother (there was not time in her watchful diligence over her husband and daughter, who eased away from it whenever they could).

Not her father—his pains were not the kind you could categorize.

Her grandmother—yes, she was sure her grandmother had headaches. And arthritis.

He was smiling and nodding, he was young, and self-important, he asked her if there was anything stressful going on in her life. She was tired, she was writing a book and teaching, well, that would be enough, certainly, and he told her about his sister who was doing a Ph.D. in Chaucer and was exhausted from it.

She left with a prescription for Ergotamine, which made her throw up even more violently with her headaches.

23

ELIZABETH, IN HER SEARCH for the Hausmanns, finds George Blackwell.

It is a hunch; she was never a methodical researcher—her habits of grasping at ideas, working on intuition, drove Greg crazy. But they often paid off. There were three George Blackwells in the Vancouver phone directory. The right one lived in Cedarglen.

George Blackwell is newly and uncomfortably retired; her visit and its implications are an obviously welcome diversion. He tells Elizabeth this as they sit in his living room with its bay windows looking out over the inlet. The house is upright, stucco, thirties vintage. The view is magnificent.

His wife brings in coffee and small chocolate chip cookies. She is wearing tight polyester white slacks; her thighs bulge through in ripples.

She tells Elizabeth how hard it is to get used to having George around all the time, instead of at the telephone office.

"The first week," George says (he has thick round glasses which accentuate his round face, his hair has thinned to a few carefully placed strands), "I was going around on cloud nine—all this time on my hands. Now, I don't know what to do with myself."

"Yes," Elizabeth says, "one of my uncles is retired now and I think he paints the house three times a year. He drives my aunt crazy..."

And has become a stalker of supermarket bargains. Their lives have contracted to a minimal level, each eyeing the other, afraid to move in case they are throttled; they have settled into a familiar pattern—he brings home groceries, she complains about them...that is their communication.

"My grandfather died when I was about eighteen—but I sure remember him. I was named after him. He was some old guy." George pulls in his coffee noisily. The phone rings; his wife goes into the kitchen. "He lived not too far from here, on the outskirts of Cedarglen, which was really just wilderness."

So it was Cedarglen. Elizabeth was not surprised.

"I grew up in Cedarglen," she says.

"Did you? This is a funny place, there are still families who've been here for a dog's age...place has changed. In my day it wasn't a Vancouver suburb—it was quite separate, but now you can't tell where the city ends and this place begins. Still, a lot of the kids I went to school with still live here and so do their sons and grandsons."

Elizabeth has told George Blackwell about the book she is writing. "Your grandfather knew the Hausmanns, the couple who were supposed to have been enemy agents..."

"He mentioned them often—it was something that bothered him. He said they were given a bum rap...in fact, he told us the story so often that after a while you didn't pay any attention any more. You know how it is. Just a story in the family."

"Do you remember why he thought they must be innocent?"

"Well, I'm not sure—there seemed to be a bunch of things. He helped the man—what was his name?"

"Tom."

"That's right—Tom Hausmann—build his boat. He said it

was the biggest thing in his life, that boat. He just said they were nice people...especially for English people who had just come out here, and who kind of looked down on Canadian things at first—" George set his coffee cup down on the wedge shaped table. "I'll tell you a funny story. My grandfather, he said the Hausmanns were real disappointed on their train ride across Canada because they didn't see any red Indians. They kept looking out on the prairies—I think they expected to see Indians riding out of the hills on horses waving tomahawks or something. That's something my grandfather used to get a kick out of..." George chuckled.

His wife was setting out another plate of cookies. She sat down. George looked at her; she was intrusive and she knew it and she stayed.

"Lots of this stuff I can't remember any more. You know how you are when you're a kid—you get sick of listening to old people—but I think he said they were kind of fancy, or they wanted to be—you know, built this little house from books and then tried to hire a maid. His wife..."

"Bess—"

"...she thought the world of her husband, that's what my grandfather said. I think Hausmann was sickly or something, and his wife she just thought the sun rose and set on him. I don't remember my grandmother hardly at all, she died when I was five, but I guess she went over to the Hausmanns and she'd say Hausmann's wife was always complaining because she couldn't get help, and I think they must have been used to having people pick up after them...But my grandfather said he got a kick out of them, even if they were snobby. He liked them—they were sort of sincere—they tried hard to fix things up. They did the best they could. My grandfather though—he was a character—kept his sense of humour all his life..."

George launched himself upon tales of his grandfather and himself—expeditions to the creek behind his property to look for small trout. George remembered climbing up the cherry tree in his grandfather's garden and how he'd make himself sick gorging.

"She doesn't want to hear about that..." George's wife, never identified, says defiantly. She is smoothing the brushed black velvet of a sofa cushion.

George ignores her. "I believed my grandfather when he said these people were innocent. And you know, I read up on it...and the whole thing stinks."

"It sounded pretty circumstantial to me. They may certainly have rammed into the *Anabelle*—there's the testimony of the cabin boy—but the idea of them being spies or saboteurs seems to be pretty far fetched. I don't know why it was bought so easily."

"It was like that in the First World War. Did you know about the lodge up the inlet? It was built by this German millionaire, he made it rustic, and his buddies and him used to be up there drinking and all—a hunting lodge I guess it was. Well, the Canadian government just confiscated it in 1915— just took the damned thing over, because he came from Germany...I mean it was unbelievable. You saw some of that in the Second World War—I didn't see much of the Germans, I was in Italy mostly...but the propaganda was unbelievable..."

"I didn't know about the lodge." (This wasn't strictly true—she knew it in its fifties reincarnation as a tourist stop at the end of a long winding beautiful ride up the inlet.)

"Hard to believe all this stuff now, isn't it?" George Blackwell was shaking his head.

"Do you know exactly where the Hausmanns lived?"

"Sure. Next door to my grandfather's house. All the people there lived on big acreages in those days. I can give you the address—in my grandfather's day there was no address, just two houses left of the gulley, that sort of thing. There's nothing left of those old houses there any more—there's a bunch of fourplexes, but part of the property is still vacant, some developer sitting on it..."

"I'll get your book when it comes out," George says to her as he lets her out. "It's about time someone wrote something about that sinking."

But I'm not writing about that sinking, Elizabeth thinks as she climbs into her car—at least that's not what I'm supposed to be doing.

The site of the Hausmann's acreage is disappointing. It is on the brow of the hill, which when Elizabeth was small was totally treed, the site of the family Christmas tree cutting. She remembered Will's saying that the Hausmanns' home had been torn down, burned, the destruction egged on by a vindictive mob. Of course there would be nothing left.

A gaudy post-modern blue and pink building with turrets added to it like afterthoughts is sprawled over cement, filled with parked cars—it interferes with the wild lot beside it, still tangled with blackberries and grass. Elizabeth walks around in the grass, careful that she doesn't catch her cotton pants on the blackberry thorns. In the middle of the lot a large dead tree—an apple tree, probably—bends itself into the sky. Elizabeth stops and looks at it—this might have belonged to Bess and Tom. The sight is pathetic, ominous like pictures she'd seen of the post-World-War-I battlefields, grass growing, but still the gnarled black sticks hanging like gibbets over the growing vegetation.

There is nothing else to suggest the Hausmanns had ever lived there. But the view they must have looked down on is intact; this far up the inlet the north shore has not been settled much, it must have been similar, and on a day like this with the sun sifted through soft clouds, it is beautiful.

They must have stopped and looked at the ocean and mountains and thought they were in heaven.

This time, Elizabeth decides to drive past her old home. She knows it is not there, of course, her mother has told her. It has been replaced by Vancouver "specials," the ubiquitous narrow two-storied boxes side by side, totally alike. Only two old houses are left in the block huddling forlornly together, one empty, its windows boarded up. The inlet below has narrowed, industries stretch into its centre, smoke belches against the mountains now half bare, pocked with houses.

Elizabeth is glad to leave the street.

Elizabeth, that night, wonders what to do with George Blackwell's testimony. There is nothing new, all confirming what she already knows.

Ursula stares down at her from the bulletin board.

The phone rings.

It is George Blackwell; she has given him her number.

"I thought of something," he says. "There was an article I saw—it must be ten years ago—about the cabin boy, Jim...he was still alive then."

"He'd be pretty old."

"Yeah, he was. He was all there though—remembered everything like it was yesterday. He was living in Vancouver somewhere, I think."

"That is interesting. He'd be the only living link..."

"Yeah, I thought you might be interested. I never kept the article, it was in the *Sun*, so you might find it..."

24

THE ARTICLE IS ON MICROFICHE at the Vancouver archives—as are other articles updating James Rowan's activities through the years. He is hailed as a hero in 1915; interviews reveal nothing that Elizabeth has not found. In 1924 Rowan appears again under the heading "Great Sinking Recalled"—he is now a mate working on the CPR boat, the *Princess Maquinna*, which served the west coast of Vancouver Island. His statements are the same as his 1915 testimony, although by now they are more elaborate, the tumult of the sinking drawn out, the meeting of Ursula and Bess Hausmann across the decks, agonized, lengthened.

There is nothing until 1940 when he volunteers (although he is now forty) for the Royal Canadian Navy, and he is en route to Halifax where he is to join a convoy escort. He recalls the First World War and the espionage off the coast.

"I never trusted the Germans," he is quoted as saying, "and I was right. They never finished what they set out to do—take over the world—and now they're going to try and do it. I saw what they were capable of doing then." There is a picture of Jim Rowan, the first one Elizabeth has seen. He is sharpfeatured, a cigarette dangles out of a corner of his mouth.

He appears once more in a brief clipping in October 1965, recalling the fiftieth anniversary of the sinking. He is retired by now, a grandfather, he lives in Vancouver's east side, in the same house in the ex-servicemen's quarters. Elizabeth knows the area—rows and rows of wooden houses exactly the same, the only variance the positioning of the front steps and porch.

He has become a model train enthusiast; the whole basement has been given over to his trains. In the accompanying photograph he is wearing a striped engineer's cap.

He says the sinking of the *Anabelle* was a long time ago. He would rather talk about the trains.

The piece George Blackwell had noticed—the copy from spring 1983—is actually disappointing in its details. It is part of a Lifestyles/Living section on great shipwrecks of the past. Jim Rowan is at this time eighty-three. Three years before, he and his wife had moved into a seniors' complex where they bought a small townhouse. They were self-sufficient there, he said, though they could join others for meals if they wished; there was a doctor and nurse available, and adjacent to the complex a building for chronic care. Both Jim and his wife were active (he is sorry he had to give up his train collection)— they go to bingo together in the big recreation room, there's a shopping complex across the street with the biggest supermarket in the city, they have a tiny strip of garden where Jim grows lettuce and tomatoes in the summer.

The interviewer asks him what he remembers of the *Anabelle* sinking and he says it was a bad business. He goes over the story but gives no new details.

Elizabeth turns off the microfiche and asks the archivist, a young woman with very short hair and a brightly patterned T-shirt, if she knows whether or not Jim Rowan, the cabin boy of the *Anabelle,* is still alive.

The archivist doesn't know, and Elizabeth decides to phone the seniors' home.

25

JIM ROWAN IS BEING WALKED TOWARDS HER. He is emaciated, his face a skull with paper skin pasted on it. The chronic care facility is depressing; the room Elizabeth stands in is bordered by a row of old people in wheelchairs or couches, most with heads slumping on their chests. It is clearly a waiting room.

The nurse says, "Mr. Rowan, here's someone to see you." She says to Elizabeth, "We'd better sit down." They are escorted to a corner of the room, where two large chairs are set in front of a television. There is a game show in progress; a half dozen women are propped up in front of the TV, but two are asleep.

"I'll leave you for a bit,"—the nurse looks at her watch—"but lunch is in twenty minutes." She says this very loudly to Jim Rowan.

"Lunch," he says. There is a small trickle of water running down the corner of his mouth. He looks at the nurse. "Lunch," he says again.

The nurse has told Elizabeth that Mr. Rowan forgets things.

Elizabeth leans forward. "My name is Elizabeth Morrison—

I'm writing a book."

"Eh?" Jim Rowan leans forward, his hand with its translucent skin cups his left ear.

"I'm writing a book," she says loudly. Two of the women propped up in front of the TV turn to look; their stares contain only a flicker of interest. The television is turned down very low—she wonders if they can hear at all.

This is not a good place to be interviewing.

"A book? I don't read very much now." His voice is husky, small, the words delivered without enunciation. "Used to. What's your name again?"

"Elizabeth."

"Do I know you?"

"No, no you don't. Actually I want to ask you what you remember about the sinking of the *Anabelle*. I'm doing a book, and this is a big part of it."

He does not answer. She wants to use a handkerchief to stop the drool which is falling onto his shirt.

"I want to..." she starts again, but he reaches his hand out and swats the air.

"I heard you...the *Anabelle*, you said."

"Yes. I'd be very grateful if you could tell me anything you remember."

"Were you there?" He looks agitated.

"No. No. I'm writing about it."

"I told them here all about it. I told them here."

"Did you?"

"*Here.*" He says it emphatically. "I used to be a mate on the CPR boats, you know."

"I know. I read about it."

"Did you. Now isn't that nice?" A smile moves along his mouth, his teeth are too large for his face.

"Spent a lot of time on this coast. Did you know Jane?"

"No."

"Jane, my wife...she's around here somewhere." (The nurse has told Elizabeth that Jim Rowan is now a widower.)

"Mr. Rowan..." Elizabeth is not sure how to proceed, "do

you remember anything about the *Anabelle*'s sinking? You were the cabin boy—in 1915..."

"Yes." He says it simply. "I was on her when she went down."

"And you remember, do you, that the small boat—the *White Swan*—had rammed the *Anabelle*?"

"Yes, she did." He was looking at her steadily now.

"So as far as you were concerned the small boat was in the wrong, making for the *Anabelle*?"

"Who told you that?"

"Isn't that what you said—in your testimony?"

"They made me say that..."

His fingers claw at his forehead.

"Who made you say that?"

"Them—the navy. The Admiral, he went down in the *Anabelle*, you know..."

"Yes, Admiral Bailey..."

"I was in the navy in the war...we were escorting convoys, and there were these U-boats...it was hard going..."

"The Second World War, you mean?"

"Yes, the second war." He turns his head slowly towards the TV set and looks at it, his mouth opening slowly.

"Mr. Rowan, you saw Ursula La Fontaine on the *Anabelle*? Do you remember her?"

"Who?" His gaze is slowly drawn back to Elizabeth.

"Ursula La Fontaine—the actress who drowned on the *Anabelle*...it was her yacht."

He nods. "She was a fine looking woman. And bossy. Everything had to be just right. It was my first trip out on that boat. She was prettier by far than the other woman."

"What other woman?"

He was frowning slightly. "The one on the other boat—"

Elizabeth pulls her chair closer. "Mr. Rowan, I've read that you saw that woman and Ursula stop for a minute and stare at each other—is that true?"

"True as I sit here. Damn shame—that poor woman, her and her husband. But then, maybe they were spies. The

Admiral, you know he tied the wheel down."

"On the *Anabelle*?"

"He tied the wheel down because they were having a high old time drinking and he was after her, married and all, after that actress on the *Maquinna*."

"Do you mean the *Anabelle*?"

He looks puzzled. "The *Maquinna*, she went aground you know, down near Sidney, there on Vancouver Island."

"But the *Anabelle*—why would the Admiral tie the wheel down?"

"Because he didn't know what the hell he was doing. He was drinking, he'd sent the captain down below—ordered him—said he was going to steer the boat. I was up in the wheelhouse, bringing them drinks, and she was with him and they were cozying up pretty good, and him married, too. That actress, she could put away the drinks herself, drank like a man...he was figuring I guess they had a smooth straight passage, and he wanted his hands free, if you get my drift..."

The smells of fried chicken are emanating from some-where.

"Lunch," he says. "I can still smell, you know." He is sniffing the air as cats do.

"Mr. Rowan," Elizabeth speaks slowly, clearly, "you're positive the wheel was tied down on the *Anabelle*?"

"True as I sit here. That bunch on board, the noisiest and drunkest bunch I ever come across, and that's counting some high times in the Navy."

"Did you ever tell that story to the press? I've never come across that."

"They come and see me in the hospital, and I told these fellows, big important fellows from the Navy, what I told you and they said I mustn't say this to anyone. To damage the reputation of the Admiral in wartime would be like handing the war over to the Germans. There was two of them—one of them was Lieutenant Taylor, I remember that because my sister, she married a Taylor—she's dead now—and I don't remember the name of the other fellow at all."

"So you never told anyone?"

"My wife, I told her. Everyone around here I tell them all the time. Nobody cares any more. It's too long ago. But the *Anabelle*, she was weaving and wandering, and me and the cook were getting scared out of our minds because we figured there would be an accident."

"The little boat then, it couldn't help hitting the *Anabelle*?"

He stares at her. "It couldn't get out of the way. It had the right of way, too..."

"But they got blamed. Mr. Rowan, the people in the little boat, they were called saboteurs..."

"Maybe they were. How would I know? They had some German name. Everyone said they were spies after the Admiral. Maybe so. I didn't know...I was just a kid. I just did what I was told. We rescued this boat, the *Norah*; I was a hand on the *Maquinna*. There were these people got stranded on Ripple Rock, the one they blew up, I saw that on the television, when they blew her up—high time, she was a danger to navigation with ships hanging up on her all the time. There were spies all over in the war. Mata Hari, she was shot, and there were spies in France. I had a ship mate on the *Invincible* and he died of a ruptured appendix out there in the middle of the Atlantic. He was my best pal at the time. Jane, my wife, she never knew him. You talk to Jane, she knows I told her about the *Maquinna*."

People are walking or being wheeled towards a huge arched doorway. The nurse is coming towards Mr. Rowan.

"Lunchtime, Mr. Rowan."

He tries to stand up, but sinks back and waits for her to help him.

Elizabeth stands up. "Thank you, Mr. Rowan," she says, "you've helped a lot."

"She was a good ship, the *Maquinna*, built in Scotland."

"I'm sure." She reaches out to shake his hand, small sticks in her grip.

"I don't remember much about that other one you were asking about." His eyes are crafty. "I may have got it all wrong."

"I'll see you again, Mr. Rowan," Elizabeth says, but when she phones again, she is told Jim Rowan has influenza and isn't talking to anyone.

❧

"They were set up; it's pretty clear." Elizabeth and Will are on the terrace at the faculty club.

"That's fascinating stuff." Will is relentlessly fingering his car keys; he is down to three cigarettes a day. "I think there's been a lot of scepticism about the wrecks, particularly the accusation against the Hausmanns, but no one ever uncovered anything. It's like the Shaughnessy murder mystery, where the maid was killed at a party—rumours of dirty doings among the toffs, but the houseboy was accused. And there's still no answer. Sixty years later."

"I know things are covered up. Who's going to blame an admiral, in wartime, of fooling around, drunk, with Ursula, or of dismissing the captain and tying the wheel down on the boat so presumably he could do even more serious fooling around? And that puts a different light on Ursula's death. The common assumption is that she was the innocent victim of a plot. It's another thing to have been posthumously involved in a plot."

"If it's true—if Mr. Rowan is accurate—then the last days of Ursula's life were spent in a drunken party."

"I'm sure it's true. He wasn't that addled. And that's not the sort of thing you'd make up. Why would you?"

"Yes, why would you? So, what's your next step?"

"I'm going to see if I can find anything out about the man who came to see Jim Rowan when he was recuperating in the hospital—Lieutenant Taylor. I'll see what I can track down."

~~❧~~

The tracking down of Lieutenant Joseph Taylor proves to be a dead end. Correspondence with the Department of National Defence turns up information that Lieutenant Taylor, stationed at Esquimalt until 1917, joined the Royal Naval Air Service and was shot down in May 1918 in the Atlantic. He had grown up in Victoria. And though Elizabeth searched diligently, there was no sign of family or relatives.

26

UNDER THE SEA, PERCEPTIONS FLOAT, waver, are unclear. Her mother sits under a sampler that says, "Home Sweet Home" though neither she nor the sampler are touched by the water, her mother who cooked stews and roasts and spaghetti and shepherd's pie and things like "mock duck" which was disguised heart, and animals' innards under assorted names. Her mother who baked wonderfully, her pies and tarts the first to go at church bazaars and at Elizabeth's school, when the nuns always said to Elizabeth: "We hope there will be more of your mother's wonderful baking." There always was.

Her mother needed, thinks Elizabeth, a domestic daughter, a child who would stand up on a stool and enjoy kneading dough and sprinkling sugar onto triangular tea scones. Elizabeth was never interested; she lived in books, in made-up scenarios, the world she saw relating to her in words, and especially in old words—old houses with ornaments, rooms with niches whose meanings were lost, the remains of a derelict boat, its bones flat against the transparent sea. Traces of people who had come and gone.

Elizabeth and her mother look at each other across enormous gulfs. Elizabeth is neatly, prettily dressed, her hair done up by her mother in rag curlers to be combed into ringlets, dresses hand sewn, pattern books and envelopes stacked neatly by the sewing machine. Her mother wanting her to be female, which meant arranging life for a husband and children, and Elizabeth resisting arrangements, deliberately, fending her mother off as one fends off menacing creatures underwater. But her mother was never menacing.

Elizabeth turned out tall and flat, slim hipped, happier in boats, on bicycles, and unable to cook anything.

Not the daughter she wanted, Elizabeth thinks—no daughter, no wife—and is annoyed with herself for thinking this.

Who made up the niches? And why did she even think she needed to fit in one?

It is easier under the sea to see these facts floating by, in sequential order, but what to do with them?

They are also the province of Bess, domestic Bess, wrongfully accused.

Who was devoted to her husband.

≈

What continued underwater were the tentacles of guilt which bound her by the throat.

Let it go. Let it all go.

≈

Her mother visiting Elizabeth in the apartment, coming for tea—she is sitting uncomfortably on the hard sofa, her pants and top matching, she says she just got through making them yesterday.

"That's a nice outfit, Mum," Elizabeth says.

Elizabeth serves tea in a white coffee pot and apologizes that there isn't a tea pot in the apartment. She serves jam tarts and raisin scones.

"Did you make these, Lizzie?" Her mother is taking small demure bits of the scones.

"No, there's a wonderful bakery on Tenth." Her mother nods, and says how tasty they are.

"And how is your book going?"

"Pretty well. There are always ends to tie up."

"I guess so." Her mother pours herself another cup of tea. "Tea's getting cold, Lizzie. These pots don't keep tea hot like the Brown Betty does."

Elizabeth puts the kettle on. "You know, Lizzie, I saw one of your books, the one on the border with all the photographs, in the book store; I told them you are my daughter...they couldn't get over it. Is the new book going to have a lot of photographs?"

"Probably not. A few pictures of Ursula La Fontaine, but not like *People of the Border*."

Her mother looks at her, tea cup in hand, and hesitates. Elizabeth knows what is coming. "Have you been in touch with Greg at all?"

Elizabeth fighting to the surface, nets of guilt drifting, lying in wait. "No, I haven't."

She fills the coffee pot up with hot water and drops tea bags into it.

"Aunt Agnes was asking for you. I told her you are so busy, I hardly see you."

Elizabeth sitting on the director's chair across from her mother. "Yes, she phoned."

"She still gets around pretty well, considering. Arthritis is bothering her sometimes. But she still gardens and she even went to Reno on the bus two weeks ago with her seniors group. She wanted me to come, but Les wasn't feeling too good and I didn't want to go. He's just in misery sometimes, Lizzie. I think maybe it's gall bladder—that's what the doctor thinks now; he's been through all these tests, and that's what it looks like. The doctor said he might have to get an operation, but he's scared about it; he's got such high blood pressure that he thinks he'll just die on the operating table. Poor Les."

Poor Les, poor clinging Les.

Supported by her mother, who had attached herself to him, and they are breathing each other's air.

Greg would have liked that. Would have liked her breath though it was slowly going now, expiring.

Shells, mussels, barnacles, floating arms attached to rocks, reaching out to attack, but safe, cossetted.

She could never do that for him. He could never do that for her.

Under the sea, men like finned sharks circling, circling. Around dutiful women.

Who said it had to be like this?

⨭

Her father had wanted to try the boat on a rough day. She found her mother sobbing into her creased apron."It was blowing up a gale, Lizzie, but there's no reasoning with him."

Her mother did not use the past tense. Was not to use it for some time. After the coast guard had searched, after it was clear he was not coming back.

The body was found. An autopsy was made. Her father had suffered a heart attack and drowned.

She preferred to think of him dying like this. The sea receiving him.

But he had gone down in her boat. She could not bear it.

꙾

After her father died—when the first emptiness had con-signed itself to the night, to dreams where her father appeared, home from a journey, completely present, the dark hair em-broidered with grey, the intense fluid sound of his voice though it was far off and multiplied like the distant chanting of monks, present, but somehow off centre, a character in a play who cannot reach the audience—there was her mother to look after. They were joined together in mutual recrimination and loss. It was Elizabeth's boat. Why didn't her mother stop her father from sailing on such a stormy day?

Words sometimes spoken, sometimes unspoken, rem-nants of grief. Her mother, with Elizabeth now away at university and working part-time in the student café, had no focus, putting on her apron like veterans in their old uniforms parading nowhere on Remembrance Day.

There was a small insurance policy, a small pension, a cousin was brought in to board. The cousin was widowed, gruff, immensely saving, arthritic. Her mother became house-keeper to the cousin, confidante; they repeated stories out of their pasts, her cousin's raucous laughter filling the room; they whispered ironic secrets, her mother was moving backwards, she was a girl, lost in her own time frame.

They became tourists. Joining the seniors groups, they toured the coast, took a bus trip to Las Vegas where they took in free shows and ate the free gravy-laden dinners.

Elizabeth found herself coming home with no one there, no dinners, no one to talk to, and the house laden with her father.

She saved enough from tutoring and a summer job as a playground director to share a dark, musty basement suite with a girl from the Newman club who said her prayers loudly at night, and who was dating a science major. They were making plans, they would be married in the summer when they graduated and it was clear Paula's Home Ec training would be directed towards the making of a home.

She would work the first year. Then she would have babies.

Paula was cheerful (especially in the morning, flicking on the bright overhead light in the bedroom and singing while she put on coffee). She was also able to concoct tasty things on the hotplate, while Elizabeth, fending for herself, opened a can.

Elizabeth was glad when Paula moved out, leaving her at last alone.

While the girls nearing graduation rushed frantically to link themselves up before it was too late, and they were truly forced into teaching or nursing, Elizabeth knew she didn't want to marry. Not in any hurry.

The cousin and her mother interviewing her. "Lizzie, now who's the young fellow came around here last week…good looking fellow, don't you think so, Margaret?" (The cousin to her mother.)

"Lizzie's always had lots of boyfriends. She's getting too hard to please; time is running out. I keep telling her that." (Her mother.)

"Girls with their noses stuck in books don't attract the fellows." (The cousin) "Remember Marion lived two doors down from us? You could see she was going to be an old maid. She was smarter than any of the boys in her class, and the boys didn't like it. Mind you, she didn't have Lizzie's looks."

∽⌒

Elizabeth was a good teacher; she received a fellowship to start her M.A. programme (research into the history of the early Empress boats and the Orient routes) and taught a first-year class. She found once she got over being nervous, could

cover herself with a podium, got wrapped up in her subject—
modern history: Bismarck to World War II—she enjoyed the
classes. Sometimes she felt there were others speaking through
her, telling stories—the bards, the orators from her people's
island, whose hard repetitive outer lives were only part of the
continuum, the other filled with confessions of ghosts and
demons, miracles and exhilaration. They had never given up
their bones to grave markers or prayer cards.

27

HER MOTHER WHEN SHE VISITED had brought Elizabeth a movie film which she said she'd had for ages. "It says 'Christmas,'" she said, "I don't know what year. I think we rented a movie camera one Christmas—in the fifties, I think."

Elizabeth didn't remember the year either, but she did remember the horrible glare of the bar lights used at the time, flooding the Christmas table with their intense, searing heat.

Elizabeth wondered if there were projectors available any more to show the film now that everyone was videotaping. There were; she found one at the large camera store two blocks from her apartment, where the clerk advised her to put her old films on videos with suitable music in the background.

She projected the film onto the white apartment wall; the stuccoed surface showed through so that the people walked amid grainy bumps, appeared under water. But the images were clear. Christmas, mid-fifties from the look of the clothes and hair, the table elongated with additional boards, holding additional relatives who wore paper hats, garish green and red crepe intensified in the glare, looking up from the turkey, frowning at the intrusion of the lights; there was no sound, of course. She was sitting beside her father—he was wearing a paper hat shaped like an admiral's, his hair sliding out from under. Elizabeth felt a pang of recognition. She wanted to turn the film off.

The spotlight was on her mother now, sinking under layers of dishes, her aunt with her dishtowel, both wearing half-aprons, her mother's "go away" mouthed with a self-conscious smile, her uncle playing the accordion, his head bent so that his ear was resting on the glossy black instrument, and then her father again, a pan shot now—who had taken this film? She had no idea. Her father, smiling, glass of whisky in his hand, the whole room now replete with whisky. What was he watching. The pan continued—she was standing in her frilly party dress, fluffed out with petticoats, and someone was taking her picture, the filmmaker taking pictures of the picture-taking. Her father was looking at her. Smiling approvingly. The film was fading, there was a wall now, her father's gaze was fading.

She shut off the projector.

Had her father always watched her like that? She felt a sense of unease. Without the sound, without the tales, the poetry that he spun so easily, he was less present. He did not belong in silent movies. She tried to remember the lyrical cadences, the overlays of irony, humour...but they had disappeared like the voices of her favourite teachers, who paced the stage and fixed glittering eyes upon the students, transfiguring them. Only the notes were left. Her father's notes she could not decipher.

28

KAREN AND ELIZABETH, PAUL AND PATRICIA are back diving on the *Anabelle*. Elizabeth has told the others about Jim Rowan. She is disappointed in the reaction. The Allenbergs are politely interested. Only Karen from the scuba shop accepts the information with excitement.

"Just imagine," she says, as they are en route to the site. The engine of the dive boat is smooth and rhythmical. The sea breeze, cool. "If that were right, it would change history."

"If I could find evidence that the wheel was tied down—is that possible?" Elizabeth is addressing Paul Allenberg.

"Well, anything's possible but a wheel would be one of the first things to be picked off—that would be a real find."

"I suppose so. That's the trouble, I know it's a long shot. And finding pieces of rope—even more unlikely, presuming the wheel was tied down with rope."

"Oh, I expect so, hemp, sea rope…it's not unusual for a wheel to be tied down, though illegal, of course."

"Yes." Elizabeth remembered a sail when the wind died down—she was a university student—the small engine putting slowly along the glass ocean, the skipper, who was in commerce and had already made a small fortune in the stock market, had tied the wheel down, put his feet up. "It can steer itself," he said. She remembers his voice, the air filled with stock quotations while the coastline thick with August went slowly by.

"If you wanted to find something like a wheel, you'd really need to know what you're doing, like the underwater archaeologists, divide the area into fields, search inch by inch. I was with a group diving on the *Lucy Anne* off Vancouver Island—they really know what they're doing, very painstaking."

"I know. And they have sonar and who knows what else. I imagine there's no chance I'll find anything—I want to look around, though—I may stumble across something…"

"Can't you just cite the testimony of the old man—a hypothesis?"

"I expect that's what I'll have to do."

"Maybe we'll find the *White Swan* today," Karen says. "You should see that boat, anyhow…"

"I *must* find the *White Swan*."

"Don't you two wander off, " Patricia warns. They have stopped now; the skipper is dropping anchor. They plan the dive. They are pulling on their wet suits, neutered suddenly, fish-shaped, amorphous.

Elizabeth is descending; she is aware of falling, of time stopping. She rolls over, is now diving head first. The water is darkening, and she is moving so slowly she thinks she is still—down, down, down the rabbit hole, will it ever stop?—she had never known a dive to take so long, and yet she feels unafraid, the ocean is lulling her, there is music from somewhere, the coral hum, the siren song beyond human ears, hidden like the high whistle only animals can hear.

She has reached the bottom; her light fastens on the *Anabelle*. Elizabeth gives Karen the OK sign and they circle the wreck. The *Anabelle* has now become familiar and thus clearer. In Elizabeth's mind the pieces have floated back together. She has seen so many pictures of the *Anabelle* she can remove the barnacles, the silt, the octopus lair, the things that leech upon her. Elizabeth tries to loosen her knife from her belt; the process is more difficult than she remembered—her gloved hand seems unable to obey her mind; she feels like a robot, some circuitry has gone wrong. And all the while she thinks that she is watching herself in an ancient silent movie, in a hollow movie house shaped like a cave or a coffin, except that the action should be fast, jerky. Her movie is shot at half speed, the frames frozen.

She is able to finally disentangle the knife and swims over to a moulded object; after a struggle she releases it from the ocean floor. It is heavy, metal of some description, nothing she is looking for; she places it back carefully where she found it. Elizabeth is reminded of the cardboard ships that came in fragments in cereal boxes when she was a child. To be folded and tucked piece into piece. That is what this movie is about: she is a child still playing a child's game, but because she is looking backward, she is sleepwalking, under the ocean. Slow, slower, slower.

Elizabeth feels kindly towards the *Anabelle*. "Everyone has stripped, raped you...I'll protect you," she says. Karen's light shines on her again. Elizabeth curls her fingers in the OK sign, and notes they will scarcely fit together. Elizabeth has seen the sketches at the Maritime Museum of other famous wrecks. They have received the full treatment—computerized and catalogued so that they can be laid out in huge blueprints, and it is clear where all the pieces have fallen.

"I'll document you, *Anabelle*," she thinks. She is feeling warm in spite of the chill water. She is overcome by her good feelings. She floats around the port hull; there is exposed planking, cement ballast. Suddenly Jim Rowan's voice, frail, soft through the water: "He tied down the wheel," and she remembers, and her light flashes on object after object, Karen following her; they are searching now. She awkwardly chooses barnacled mounds, but cannot remove them; she thinks there is nothing that suggests a wheel, or portion of it, and the ocean is full of filaments that might be ancient ropes broken up and floating forever. She does not care, she is so content, soporific, she could sleep...she fumbles with her knife, sees Karen's light poking the darkness.

She beckons to Karen, they descend towards the stern of the *Anabelle*, float around the rusted boiler with its ribbons of seaweed, the steam engine frosted with sea anemones, the cylinders holding more treasure of kelp. She has intruded upon a party, someone has turned the lights out, and the ocean is filled with languid excitement. Elizabeth and Karen float up, as they have arranged, in the direction where they have already looked for the *White Swan*.

Their lights disturb gaping fish, sponge forests, lawns of smooth rocks, but there is no sign of the *White Swan*.

Bess should be somewhere near by. If the *White Swan* had rammed the *Anabelle*, surely they went down close together, entangled, Karen said she had seen the ship. They should be close together.

Bess and Ursula. Face to face.

Elizabeth scans the ocean bottom, small floating objects move around her like snowflakes on a dark night. There is no sign of the alien pieces that might be the *White Swan*.

She checks her regulator, her time; she has enough air. She has nearly five minutes. Behind her Karen is giving her the sign that she wants to go up, and Elizabeth shakes her head. She has no intention of going up yet, she is ready to burst into song. She is reaching for stones on the ocean floor, but they elude her grasp...Karen points up again, and gives a danger sign, but there is no danger, the dark waters are comfortable, gentle. Elizabeth wants to laugh, but the clumsy apparatus in her mouth is in the way; she fumbles with it. Paul Allenberg is beside her; he pushes her mask back into her mouth and gives the closed fist sign: group up. Elizabeth is feeling limp, a Salvador Dali figure draped over his arm. She is ready to ascend. They are moving upwards. Her head begins to clear.

It takes forever to get to the surface. The obligatory decompression stops are endless—Karen is beside her, watching her, the water lightens, she can see again. Her exhaustion is so great, she can barely hand her weight belt to the skipper. Paul and Patricia, already on board, help her with the tanks. She is pulled up the ladder, and collapses on the deck.

Paul is beside her. "Are you all right?" he asks.

"Fine," she says, "exhausted—what happened down there?"

"I think it must have been narc—nitrogen narcosis. Has this ever happened to you before?"

She pulls herself up on her elbows, "Not so bad—I remember a couple of times thinking I had no co-ordination, my reflexes were off, but nothing like this."

"It happens." The skipper is bringing out the hot coffee. "Sometimes how you ate, how you slept—or didn't sleep— will determine whether this comes on."

"I didn't sleep much last night. A few hours, I think." Another night of hot tubs and nightmares.

"That'll do it. I remember once after hardly any sleep, I was down there, tying and untying this knot and singing to myself. I didn't even know why I was doing it. It's a good idea at that point to come up."

"That's one of the scary things," Elizabeth says. She is still in her wet suit; she is going to keep it on till she warms up. "I didn't think I needed to come up."

"That's why you've got a buddy," Patricia says. She is reassuring, matter-of-fact. She reminds Elizabeth of a childhood friend who had mothered everyone in the neighbourhood.

"It's one of the perils of deep diving—you haven't done so much of it, I take it? Not in cold water, anyway," Paul says.

"No. In the Caribbean, mostly."

"You can see why they call it rapture of the deep; you do get drunk. There are all the stories, apocryphal or not—divers giving their masks to fish, cutting hose lines…it might be a good idea to use a buddy line with Karen. This is so much colder and darker than the Caribbean. Diving deep down there is a shoe-in compared to the west coast."

"I was diving once with this guy,"—Karen is bringing Elizabeth more coffee—"up the arm of the inlet. It was deeper than this. He got weird like you did...I had a time getting him to come up. But he went down another time and nothing happened. I think as you get used to deep diving here, it gets better."

"I'm going to keep on." Elizabeth drains the coffee. She is out of the wet suit, in sweat pants and flannel top; she pulls on thick socks—her feet are still cold. "A few more dives...I want to see the *White Swan*. It's vital."

"Why?" Patricia in her shorts and hooded sweatsuit has returned to normal; they have all returned to normal, male and female. Elizabeth feels warm, surrounded, one of them.

"It's simply necessary to see the *White Swan*—it's the last footnote for the book. If I can't find the wheel, and I'm sure I can't, I must see the remains of the *White Swan*."

"I think we've about done with the *Anabelle*," Patricia says. "In two weeks, Paul and I were thinking of going up to the Sechelt Peninsula, off Tranquil Island. There's two wrecks, not too old, the twenties, but there's a lot of stuff to see. You're all welcome."

"I've dived on those wrecks," Karen says. "It's wonderful. One of them is huge, a freighter, and you suddenly come across her—it's fantastic; I had to back up to see all of it. You'll have a great time."

Elizabeth says she wouldn't be joining them. She asks Karen if she is willing to come back to the *Anabelle*. "Sure, not this weekend, next. You've got me curious now—I *know* I saw that other boat."

29

ELIZABETH SEES BESS AGAIN. After diving—she thinks it was after diving—and now, for the first time, Bess speaks to Elizabeth.

— *We weren't spies*. She says it simply, directly.

— *I know*, Elizabeth says.

Because the presence of Bess is so overwhelming, Elizabeth expects her words to be memorable, as voices in dreams, ordinary words freighted with unbearable decisions. But she is very ordinary. Bess says: *We were patriotic English people, we believed overwhelmingly in the British Empire, even in Canada we were aware we were British.*

Elizabeth is surprised that Bess is speaking in her time. Speaking of Empire.

— *I know you were patriotic*, Elizabeth tells her. They are meeting again underwater. Bess, as before, is wearing the long automobile coat, but her head now is uncovered, her hair long, unpinned.

— *Tom and I loved Canada, because it was part of the Empire. We particularly loved the west coast, though I must admit it was overwhelming at first. When we decided to buy our acreage it was in the midst of the forest, looking over the inlet, looking across to the mountains. In a spot that had no name.*

— *It was called Cedarglen, later,* Elizabeth says.

— *Tom loved homesteading. I had never seen him happier. His health had been a matter of concern; he had had rheumatic fever when he was a child and it weakened him. We decided almost immediately after we married that we could come out to Canada. Tom's cousin had come to Vancouver, and then moved up the coast to a small town, Bella Coola — the names on the coast were enchanting — though he went back to England because his wife was homesick. Tom's cousin never stopped singing the praises of the Canadian wilderness and its health-giving effects.*

We decided to settle near Vancouver, so we might have the amenities of a city near by, but still be in the country.

We moved to Canada in 1912; the ship journey was rather frightening, because we were crossing in May, not too long after the Titanic *had sunk, and we all came on deck to see where they thought she might have gone down. Even then, in May, there were icebergs, like shimmering castles all around us.*

The train ride took so long. I couldn't believe the size of the country.

It was then that I had a wave of homesickness. I questioned to myself the rightness of our decision, but Tom was so happy, so joyfully looking forward to working with his hands. You see, he was of an artistic bent; as well, he was good with numbers and measurement though as it turned out I kept all the household accounts. Tom liked to build, and we were lucky in that a spot for a house had already been cleared — the owners of the land had intended to build — and Tom could start in right away.

But I insisted we have a proper cottage. Our neighbour, George Blackwell, who introduced himself immediately and in spite of rough manners was extremely helpful, had built a small log cabin, and I wanted none of that.

It must be a cottage, like the Devon cottages by the sea, I told Tom, and he was quite amenable.

I was to learn a good deal very quickly; there were no plans available for such cottages, not the kind I was thinking of. Perhaps the centuries adding to these cottages had given them the patina I wanted. In a fit of impatience, Tom sent away to his brother, who found a book of plans and the very cottage, the plans arriving two months later. The book was called Country Homes, How to Build, Decorate, Furnish and Equip Them at an Inclusive Cost; *Tom waited for the plans fuming, laying in stocks of wood for the winter, helping me plot a garden.*

George Blackwell found the cottage plans amusing, telling us that was all right in the old country, but would look silly here.

I don't think so, I said, and I didn't care if it did.

The next lesson I learned was that it is very difficult to live in a tent. And that is where we were to spend the summer months. Luckily we had sent on some of our things and had a nice mattress, blankets, and a lamp; we kept a small cook stove outside the tent, and for the most part were blessed with lovely weather. On the rainy days, it was quite miserable and I became used to donning my mackintosh and going for walks or preparing my garden, which would be my responsibility.

I would not allow myself to look back. I kept up correspondence with my family, partly because the Canadian goods were often so unsatisfactory and I wanted things sent from Liberty's and Harrod's and Fortnum and Mason. The family were dears—there was a constant stream of supplies, ribbons, jumpers, overalls, material, medicines—we found we needed laxatives often, from so much soft food. We lived on bread and jam and tinned meat—everything so costly—bread sixpence. This condition was righted once the garden grew.

Bess pauses.

—*It must have been difficult for you,* Elizabeth says, and only then when Bess looks at her, her hands folded in a demure nun-like gesture and registers no response, does Elizabeth realize that this is not a two-way conversation.

—*The house was finished at the end of August. It was a dear little house; Tom was so proud of it and I was ecstatic. Tom had some help, of course—George Blackwell joined in, and we often had trades people, who charged such exorbitant prices—you could scarcely credit. All the prices: butter two shillings a pound, Sunlight Soap five pence, jam one shilling per pound—it was hard not to think in terms of British money. Our supplies were brought by boat, though we could after a long hike take the streetcar into Vancouver. It was not convenient to carry supplies back, and indeed, there was no saving on prices.*

To get back to our house—it was spacious enough, the sitting room running through the middle, one bedroom and kitchen on one side, and two small rooms on the other. One for a spare room, and one for stores.

All around us there were explosions as people cleared their land. It sometimes made me stop my ears it was so loud.

Once the house was finished and settled, and we had scoured Vancouver for the most reasonable furniture, Tom set himself the task of building a boat. A good-sized boat. We had purchased a small boat—twelve feet—from George Blackwell, scarcely more than a rowboat with a small sail.

Tom at this time was so altered from the cautious, tentative man I had married that it was unbelievable. He had become an outdoorsman, tanned, his hands roughening—mine too, I'm afraid, though I sent over to my mother for Pacquin's lotion. Tom was full of optimism and cheer.

— *What about you?* Elizabeth bursts out. *Were you happy?*

— *I was happy to see him so happy,* Bess says, but Elizabeth knows she is not answering her question, *and though I sometimes longed for more entertainment—we visited Vancouver scarcely at all, once to see Caruso singing at the beautiful Pantages theatre, once to see the actress Sarah Bernhardt performing in* Camille—*I put all these things out of my mind and concentrated on making a home for my husband.*

— *How could you put yourself in second place?* Elizabeth says. *What about your ambitions—what did you want to do?* Elizabeth in her anger wants to shake Bess, but Bess continues, her voice harmonious, full of constrained melody.

— *I was determined in spite of the lack of help, and the inadequacy of Canadian goods, to create the kind of life that I had known. Therefore, Tom would have two lives: his boisterous, bluff life as an outdoorsman, tree cutter, angler, and his home life as an English gentleman. I created a corner for Tom—a Morris chair with his pipe stand beside it, a footstool I purchased at a used furniture store and covered with grey ticking from Harrod's. I believe I was part of the corner I created. I became increasingly adequate as a cook, much to the delight of my aunt who visited in early 1914.*

"How you get by on such little help I do not know," she said. She was talking about Clara who was my help at the time, though, like many of the others, an indifferent help. I find Canadian girls much too independent, and with no sense of a home. Clara seemed so surprised that Tom and I dressed each night for dinner, and that I expected candles on the dinner table. She was rather impudent once and I had to give her a dressing down. I had to dismiss two girls who were layabouts, and had no sense of place. I longed for the cheery domestics of England, dear England.

George Blackwell helped Tom build the boat; it was slow, slow work, beginning with the construction of a boat shed, a rather flimsy-looking affair, which Tom was very proud of. As ivy grew around our cottage, and almost into it, and I planted love-lies-bleeding, holly-hocks, lavender—seed packages which my sister obtained from Mr. Jones, the gardener who tended to all our gardens in London—the boat started taking place.

I must digress here. As I learned to cook—with the aid of Mrs. Beaton's Cook Book, the girls were useless, they could scarcely do the washing up—I began to take a great pleasure in using our produce: putting up tomatoes, making strawberry and raspberry jam. My garden was so beautiful, I had cutting flowers well into autumn and lettuce, tomato, cabbage, potatoes—all manner of wonderful fresh vegetables. I became expert at cooking fish which Tom brought me— they are so abundant one scarcely needed to sit for hours in the inlet. But to get back to Tom's boat...there was the keel, a heavy piece of oak, lying stretched out in the boat house, then the steaming of the wood for ribs, so that it might be supple and could be turned. Tom invented things—a small black stove he purchased from a touring junk man, a kettle, a hose, pipes—all for the steaming, and quite complicated.

The building took three years; Tom could not work continuously, and indeed, there was a lot of other work to do—also, he became ill twice with a terrible fever, a flu, I believe, in each case, and I was grateful for the drops of tincture of belladonna which my mother had sent and the cascara cough medicine and balsam ointment.

But he fought his way to health. I was very concerned and wondered if perhaps it was all too much for him.

— Was it too much for you? Elizabeth asks.

— Now I know it was what was keeping him alive. His new adventure, the building of the boat, a boat large enough to tour the coast, to bring supplies from Vancouver, even, and — this was my thought — to entertain any visitors we might have.

We christened her in October 1915. George Blackwell was present. We had a bottle of champagne — Tom had brought it from Vancouver months before for this purpose — and because the champagne was so precious we did not break it over her prow. We broke a bottle of ginger beer, and drank the champagne. That is, George and Tom drank most of it — I had a small glass, because it went up my nose and caused me to sneeze.

We named her the White Swan *recalling the park near Tom's home in London with the elegant swans always floating, undisturbed by crowds. I laughed at the name and told him it sounded like a pub in a provincial town.*

I must tell you (but it is not Elizabeth she is telling) *that Tom had been terribly disturbed by the news of war, more so when he knew he could not be taken for service because of his health. He had in mind that his boat perhaps could be commandeered for some useful wartime purpose though what purpose he could not tell.*

There were great parades of men joining up. George Blackwell was too old, but he said he would have gone. Not too far away, at Hastings Park, men were drilling, and women were joining Red Cross corps. I longed to do something. Mrs. Blackwell I have not mentioned because though she was kind, I found her rather offensive. The bluffness which suited George did not suit her, and her high-pitched voice and rough manners were quite appalling. There were no close women neighbours to form a sewing circle with, but I volunteered for Red Cross knitting and began to knit scarves, then socks, then sweaters, all from patterns, and after much struggle. I had never knitted in my life.

Distressing news of violence done to the Hausmann shop in

London came to us. Tom felt livid with outrage and yet powerless —
"That they could think that — my family are more loyal than those
whose families extend back hundreds of years." And indeed, the
Hausmanns were more English than the English.
    I tried to console him. It is only hysteria, I said, it will pass...
When it is understood, they will know we could never be spies.

❧

Bess has told these things to Elizabeth, or Elizabeth knows
them all at once, as knowledge is given in dreams. She knows
when she looks at Bess, words radiating like the circles of a
whirlpool, though the centre is still.

Bess is exact in her telling, as Elizabeth knew she would be.
There is no trace of self-pity.

And yet at the end Elizabeth is exhausted. She feels as if she
has been struggling with Bess, against Bess. Against the
senselessness of her life, drowned in Tom. She would have
liked Bess to have known that.

But something else is intruding.

30

HER FATHER. SHE KNOWS SHE has mythologized his image. The counsellor made that abundantly clear. The risk taker. Icarus. Flying too close to the sun.

If he were alive today and young he would have been soaring in hang gliders, windsurfing. Diving.

He would have been diving. He loved the sea because of its proximity to disaster, the edge tipping over at any moment, the ships iced over in Alaska so that they looked like pieces of a Christmas window, the storms that sent the ships on roller coaster rides, sightings of other wrecks mangled and disappearing.

(The long, boring watches, the days of playing cards in a stifling cabin, of sleeping on hard bunks, with others who might fill the cabin with sweating and farting—these were another story. Which he seldom told.)

He would have been diving.

It had begun as a good summer. Elizabeth found a job as a playground director working in a Cedarglen park, which meant she worked from noon till nine at night; no work when it rained—those days were special, when she and the other playground director, a student from the music department, sat in the clubhouse eating Peak Frean chocolate cookies and listening to old opera records.

The sunny days were filled with screaming kids with cut knees and with baseball teams of ten-year-old boys fighting on buses, craft tables knocked over by dogs, and assorted tots falling into the wading pool. But because the job was outdoors and structured and a pause between university terms, Elizabeth was filled with joy that summer; she became tanned, lithe, and developed a voice like a bull moose.

On holidays there was the sailboat. It had rested under canvas in the back yard; Elizabeth uncovered it, scrubbed it down, and repainted the name "Lizzie M." on its white hull, tracing the fading letters carefully with black paint. She varnished the mast and jib, and then she and her father towed it to a launch site on the inlet, at the base of a grassy park, and put it in the water, sailing it up under the bridge, feeling the first tug of summer, as the water warmed and the winds blew comfortably, so that they did not have to use the Seagull engine. It was at these times that Elizabeth knew she came from sea people.

They tethered the boat below the house where the shacks of the squatters huddled along the railway tracks; the caretaking of the *Lizzie M.* was given over to a grizzled beachcomber for a few dollars a month, and Elizabeth and her father made their excursions. And now more and more Elizabeth sailed alone, though her mother fussed over the idea—she didn't trust the boat.

Her mother never sailed in it; never even made the long walk down the dirt path from their house to the ocean, slippery sometimes, consumed with ferns and wild brambles. She was content to watch the ocean from their porch, to skip with her eyes from its currents and tides, to the tranquil mountains across, still mostly bare of houses. "They're very peaceful," she would say.

Elizabeth remembers a particularly windy day that summer, the sudden swoop sideways, and her gasps—"It's great,

Lizzie, hang on!"—the boat shooting through the waters as if it were riding rapids, and her fear suddenly abating, turning to delight as they rushed into the waves. Until the waves were so high that they were filling the boat and Elizabeth begged to go back. She was surprised by the reluctance of her father— when she thought about it later, she knew she shouldn't have been surprised.

(Greg and Elizabeth. In the early days, the turbulent ocean, their bodies surging, flying, the ecstasy of the last spasms, the slow quietening of the sea's pitch.)

Everything was heightened that summer.

It was too stormy for him to go out, her mother had said. Elizabeth had driven to the playground that day; it was Saturday, half-day work. She'd had her driver's license for six months—driving was still an adventure. She had the family car, a 1956 Ford; what she remembered were the tools her father kept in the trunk rattling when she went over bumps.

And she remembered the August storm, whipping up suddenly, creating frothy whitecaps, bending over trees, the wind slashing at the car windows.

Her mother had said to her, "I don't think you should take the car in this storm, Liz, it's terribly wet. You're not that good a driver yet."

Her father saying, "Don't be silly, Margaret. She's a good driver now. Go, go, Lizzie. Have a good time."

But it was her father who had gone. Out into the storm.

31

ELIZABETH IN THE ROUND BED remembers the drowning. She says the word *drowning*; it is not a metaphor. Her father had drowned. She sits up in bed. The walls are hard against her back.

"How did you feel, Elizabeth, when your father was drowned?"

"I was devastated—how would I feel?"

"Was that all?"

"Of course."

Elizabeth props the pillow behind her; her hands are clutching the white spread. It was not all; beyond the devastation, a feeling she could not examine.

"How did you feel, Elizabeth?"

"In some ways—I felt as if I were freed."

As if I were freed.

It was disloyal, sinful, wrong.

She pushes the feeling away and weeps uncontrollably, her face buried in the humped pillows till she feels she will suffocate and go under.

32

IT IS LATE AUGUST. ELIZABETH is aware of a sense of urgency; her summer is running out. Her book sits in volumes of paper bound with elastic bands, in computer disks. It has no ending. Elizabeth tells herself that she will take just one more dive. Whatever the outcome, she will finish this book.

She is diving with Karen.

They are diving at slack tide, when the water is neither coming or going. At this time of the year the currents in the Gulf can be dangerous. The waters become murkier, the plankton bloom surrounds Elizabeth and Karen so they are in a fog, even in shallower depths.

Above them, the same patient skipper reads his comic books, and waits.

Elizabeth is tied to Karen with a ten-foot buddy line looped loosely around their wrists, so they will not stray far from each other. This is difficult for Elizabeth; she is not used to being so circumscribed under the ocean.

She would rather dive alone.

In the descent, she checks for signs of nitrogen narcosis, opens and closes her free hand, reaches for her mask, her movements are instant, sharply executed. There is no sign of the rapture of the deep.

They have reached the bottom. In the wake of their lights, cloud sponges give up small rockfish, she has been told a clump as large as a person must be hundreds of years old.

She is among them, the old sponges, the ones that were there when Ursula and Bess descended.

They begin with the *Anabelle*. The water is now so dark it might be night, the lights picking up the crumpled remains of the *Anabelle*'s wheelhouse do not pierce the thick blackness.

Elizabeth shines the light on her compass; her movements are quick, unhampered. She tugs at Karen and pulls her towards the northwest, the area they have been searching.

But they find nothing. Karen is cold, Elizabeth does not linger, they ascend, still joined together, stopping at the dive rope, purging themselves for the upper world.

In the dive boat, Karen says how good it is that Elizabeth is all right this time.

Elizabeth is dissatisfied. They agree on one last dive next week. "Positively the last," Elizabeth assures Karen. "I've got a deadline."

❧

Elizabeth had not thought she would hear from Ursula. She knew finding Bess she was drifting away from Ursula. The pivot, the centre. Sometimes she saw the three of them, herself included, swirling as in a vortex, around and around. Held fast, but moving rapidly.

Not Ursula, surely. Elizabeth has been thinking about Ursula, how she might conclude her, how tenuous her grasp, once so sure, now seemed. And yet Ursula had lived her life freely, unchained to the standards of her time. Elizabeth needed to keep things in perspective. It was Bess who had been chained, whose life centred around the needs of her husband. But Elizabeth was finding it harder to define all this. It had been quite clear at one time.

There is now a tug-of-war between Ursula and Bess. Ursula has spoken to Elizabeth indirectly, evasively, as Elizabeth is coming to believe she lived her life. In a series of attitudes and poses, wrapped around now this idea, now another. It is clear, however, that she does not wish her biography to be sullied.

In a dream she speaks to Elizabeth from a portrait—she is static, dressed for a costume ball as a French aristocrat of the late 1700s, in the time before the Revolution, when the position of the aristocracy was quite clear and unassailable. Her gown is low-cut, shimmering, a hat with elaborate feathers tilted over her eye, she smiles at Elizabeth, her presence is overpowering, she speaks though there is no movement of her lips, and Elizabeth is not sure what she is saying. Only her presence, static, beautiful, conveys the message: "I am what I appear now, or what I choose to be. My life is lived with integrity and heroism. I do not wish it to appear otherwise." It is a royal command. A message from the queen, to be conveyed through the court secretary.

She is also suggesting the unimportance of the life of Bess Hausmann.

ॐ

Elizabeth receives a phone call from her editor.

It is familiar. "I don't want to put any pressure on you, Elizabeth, it's just a query to see how you're coming along."

"I'm getting there."

"Again, I don't want you to think this is cast in stone, but we were hoping to see the manuscript in say, a month—the fifteenth of September..."

"I'll try. I'm having some trouble wrapping it all up."

"When I spoke to you last, you were nearly finished..."

"It's the drowning. There's been some new information come to light—the story has been that the *Anabelle* was rammed by a small boat bent on sabotage, after the admiral who was aboard. The spy business doesn't seem to hold up, and there's some reason to believe that the ramming was the fault of the *Anabelle*, living it up on board, and not knowing what they were doing."

"Really?" The editor's voice is bland. "Does this make a lot of difference? I suppose it does. She would therefore die rather ingloriously."

"The trouble is, I don't know if I can prove it. I have the word of the cabin boy, and I believe him, but he is tending to mix things up now, and I'm not sure if others would believe him. I think it was covered up right from the start. But seventy-odd years later, it's a little hard to uncover it."

"Could you simply suggest it as a hypothesis? With evidence you found?"

"I may have to."

"It sounds fascinating. I'll leave it to you. I'm certainly anxious to see the manuscript. I'm excited about this. If we're looking at a spring publishing date—say, April—we need to get things underway."

"Wouldn't fall be better—Christmas sales, et cetera?"

"Well, yes, of course, but this would be our big book of the spring, not so much competition...people still read in spring and summer."

Elizabeth later thinks, as she did often, of getting an agent—letting someone else untangle times and rights and especially money seemed eminently sensible.

She is feeling pressured now. It is time to go back to the manuscript and tackle Ursula, try to get Ursula's life in perspective. Whatever her death, she had had a remarkable life.

She spends an evening re-reading her work. It is orderly, systematic, even dramatic. The events leading inexorably to the finale. But it is the finale that is troubling, what she had written in the last little while, here on the coast, does not fit, the sureness of the earlier part has given way to a hesitancy. The portrait of Ursula, dominant and overpowering, the woman who took, was being blurred. It is as if two different people were writing this book, and the subjects were also different.

Elizabeth sits in her apartment, with Ursula looking down from the billboard, in the background the mountains looking down on the city, the sea, and feels dissatisfied.

33

ELIZABETH DRIVING BY KITSILANO BEACH. Cool grey sky, flecks of rain, the sand undulating in waves, broken by an occasional log, almost deserted—except for a handful of dog-walkers. At anchor, the big ships motionless, flattened against the backdrop of mountains. She slows the car. She knows this beach. There were excursions out of Cedarglen to city beaches. Fish and chips and coke or orange crush, sand gritting in your teeth, the cold water, the sea breeze that made you shiver and pull your towel around you, then flop on your stomach to burn enough to go back in the water.

Fish and chips: not the uniform shoestring fries, pale and hard and inedible, but fat chips that oozed potato, all sizes and shapes, edged with golden batter. Her father bringing fish and chips home on Friday night, the oven on, waiting to keep them warm, the smell of vinegar, the half-burned newspapers cocooning them in the oven.

A concession stand is open. Elizabeth parks. She has no jacket; the mist is chilling. Behind the counter a teenager in a sweatshirt that says "Surf City, USA" looks up from his book.

"I was thinking of closing," he says. "Whatcha like?"

"Fish and chips."

"Cod? Halibut?"

"Halibut, not too many chips."

The fat sizzles. Elizabeth thinks of cholesterol again, and thinks to hell with it. The fish and chips are delicious; she soaks them with vinegar, softening the crispy batter.

She eats in the car, suddenly feels surrounded, comforted— she is in her own place, the curving ceiling with the windows that look out on an almost empty scene. And the fact that she can move away from it, invent another place, wash out the sea, the mountains, replace them with something else.

I've needed this—time alone, she thinks. She sips at her styrofoam coffee and closes her eyes, breathing deeply, relaxing. But she does not relax—behind her closed eyes her family movie continues. "Damn," she says in exasperation. The mist has slowed. A man walks by, close to the car; he is leading a little girl, a toddler, who is in a harness like a puppy; the man wears a blue jogging suit, walks slowly, stoops constantly to the child, who picks up a stone, chases a pigeon, makes sure her father follows her pointing finger.

The child is tethered to the father.

A conversation with the counsellor: she had asked Elizabeth if she ever resented being tethered to her father.

"What do you mean, _tethered_?" Elizabeth snaps.

The counsellor picks up her gold pen, a gesture that Elizabeth recognizes—she is trying to elicit a response, digging.

"From all you've told me," she says, "you had an extremely heightened relationship with your father, which I believe you're repressing. You need to let it go, but you can't until you face it." The counsellor is small; she wears a yellow suit, her waistline made minuscule with a large white belt. She speaks evenly, carefully, as if there are many words to choose from, discard.

"Heightened?" Elizabeth feels an implied criticism.

"You have such _guilt_...think about it—is it his death?"

"I don't know..."

"How about his life—you told me you felt responsible for seeing that he was happy. Isn't that a heavy burden for a child?"

"I don't think that's what I told you. I just knew his moods—I felt so good when he was happy..."

"And not good when he wasn't. You were somehow responsible."

"I don't know. No, I don't think it was quite *responsible*— we were just very close."

"Too close?"

Elizabeth remembers looking up indignantly. "What are you insinuating...something weird? Abuse? Are you trying to suggest something like that?"

The counsellor leans towards her, visibly takes a deep breath. "Why would you think of that? Why did you think I was suggesting something like that?"

"The papers are full of that kind of thing. Friends of mine— men—have said they're leery of being too friendly with children of their friends; one doesn't dare."

"Elizabeth, I'm interested in your linking here. Abuse— there is abuse which is not physical, the creation of a relationship which becomes, let's say, *emotionally* incestuous."

Elizabeth stands up. "It wasn't like that at all. That's the trouble—there are all these theories nowadays—one can't be close to a parent. This is a waste of time." Elizabeth wants to get out because she knows she is going to cry.

"I'm sorry you feel that way." The words in their calm attack Elizabeth as she walks out the door.

Elizabeth drives, not to the apartment, but to her office, where she sits, the door closed, and cries.

The terrible accusations against her father sting her. Then she tells herself that the woman's head is filled with the latest psychological junk, just like the doctors who touted a disease, an aberration of the month—osteoporosis, high blood pressure, high cholesterol—too many experts who were not human, who got their information from bulletins, pharmaceutical companies, and seminars. Not people.

She had abandoned that counsellor for the ardent feminist, one who understood women's problems and saw the real reason for her difficulties—her marriage.

The tethered father and daughter are returning now, but the child is being carried, her arms around her father's neck.

Elizabeth feels an odd blend of resentment and anger.

34

ELIZABETH IS VISITING HER AUNT AGNES. Her aunt has also invited her mother, but her mother and Les have gone to Bellingham, just over the border, for groceries and gas.

Her aunt's suite is on the main floor of a three-story thirties apartment. "Very handy," she says to Elizabeth. "I can walk out the door and get the bus." It is in Cedarglen, but away from the view.

Her aunt lives amid accretions: doilies, fringed cushions and plates that say Banff, 1948; the furniture is buried beneath what would be called "collectibles."

They have tea and butterhorns. Her aunt's face has leathered into fine lines which crisscross each other. Her eyes are crystal blue, bright against the hair that is now completely white. She must have been very pretty once; Elizabeth can't remember. She is round like Elizabeth's mother, her older sister.

"I can't cook like your mum," Auntie Agnes says, wiping powdery icing off her lips. "She just has a way with the kitchen. Actually, I don't cook too much any more. I'm getting Meals-on-Wheels which is handy, a good hot dinner every-day. You're looking well—I expected from what Margaret said you were all skin and bones. She says you're working real hard on your book."

"I am."

Her aunt sips her tea, and fans her mouth with her hand. "This is hot, mind you don't burn yourself...your husband, then, he's not with you?"

"No, he's not."

"Ah, well, what will be will be. He seemed like a nice man, the few times I met him."

"Yes, he is."

"Here, Lizzie, let me get you some more butterhorn. Here—now, you just take this." Over her protestations, another butterhorn is shovelled on to her plate. "You don't have to worry about the calories—not someone skinny like you are. Like your dad—that side of the family. You're so much like him, Lizzie..."

"Everyone says that."

"He was a charmer, your dad. Half the women around had a crush on him. Me included." She smiles at Elizabeth; she has gaps in her bottom teeth.

"On the other hand, I had a good life with Tony. He was rock solid—well, you knew him." Her Italian uncle, who brought multitudes of relatives and a men's clothing store into the family.

"He was a nice person." Elizabeth is breaking the butterhorn into tiny pieces. Her aunt has placed a butter dish in front of her, but she ignores it.

"Your dad, God rest his soul, he was a handful. I think he was too smart—you know, too smart for the kinds of jobs he had. They weren't—you know—what's the word I'm looking for...?"

"A challenge?"

"A challenge—that's what I mean. I felt sorry for your mother sometimes—I mean, she always knew the two of you were close as two peas in a pod, big imaginations—she always felt left out..."

Elizabeth looks at her aunt.

"It was a funny mix up of a marriage, in some ways...here, let me fill up your cup again...but I think he would have picked her out, anyway. Mind you, and I don't mean disrespect to the dead—it didn't hurt that my mother and father bankrolled him—you know, for his own company—what was it—you know, drawing those plans?"

"Draughting."

"That's right." Her aunt laughed. "Not that he made a go of it. But it was like what some of the foreigners do—a dowry. I'll tell you the truth, Lizzie, though, and I've never said anything to you, but I think he kind of put a burden on you...I don't know, but you can't expect kids to be adults. The sun rose and set on you—it's like only you had to make him happy. I said to Margaret that I didn't think it was fair."

"What did she say?"

"You know how she is—she keeps everything inside, she always did even when she was a kid—not like me, big blabber mouth. All she said was that she did the best she could."

Elizabeth is silent. Her aunt looks at her and says, "It's all water under the bridge, isn't it? And you've done so well—ah, well, the older I get the more I think we don't any of us know what we're doing, just wandering around trying to figure things out. I'm sure glad you came to see me."

∽

Elizabeth is looking out the window at the last bits of fluorescent sun sinking into the ocean. The sky is illuminated.

Her aunt has given her a box of cookies; they are too sweet, Peek Freans with icing on them, but Elizabeth is nibbling at them anyway.

The counsellor had told her to get rid of her father's memory.

Let it go.

She had advised Elizabeth to write a letter to him, and say what she wanted to say and then forget it.

At the time, she had thought the idea silly, the latest kooky psychology theory.

Now she is writing the letter.

She is trying not to think. To let the words come.

Dear Father, she writes.

I miss you. No one was as good to me as you were—she stares at the sentence and crosses it out. *Where are we all going? My mother. Greg.*

What have you done to me?

Had she really written that last line? It is an echo of the Good Friday Service, the lamentations—the bleak accusations poured out in the bare, dark church, the altar stripped.

She stares at her letter. She does not know what to do with it—she crumples it up, and then unfolds it again, and smooths it out with her hand.

And she knows it is her father who is drowning her.

∽

Elizabeth is meeting her mother for lunch. They are in the lunchroom of the Hotel Vancouver—Elizabeth's treat. The hotel is one of the few buildings Elizabeth recognizes in this part of town; the art deco Medical–Dental building has gone, the Edwardian Birks Building, the Hotel Devonshire, with its frosted cornices leaning over the windows—all blown up. And the towering faceless columns of glass filling the sky, crowding out the mountains.

Her mother is wearing a pink cotton suit.

"Did you make the outfit?" Elizabeth asks.

"Oh, no, I bought it—at Eaton's. The Surprise Sale—you know…"

Summer is over. The remorseless searchlight of autumn is

on their faces. Her mother has wisps of white hair under her chin; her eyes are lost in deep pouches. A glimpse of her own face looks back at her from the mirrored column—Elizabeth barely recognizes herself.

They order a bottle of wine, an expensive French white; Elizabeth's mother demurs, but Elizabeth insists. They have two glasses before their lunch—seafood quiche.

"Mmmm, this is tasty." Her mother is smiling at her. She seems almost shy.

"The crust isn't as good as yours."

"How is the book coming along?"

"Getting there."

"It's a lot of work. I told your aunt that—those books are a lot of work. They don't realize, you know."

"I suppose not."

Her mother is on her third glass of wine. "You look tired, Lizzie," she says.

"I am. I'll be glad when this is finished."

"Will you go right back to Calgary then?"

"I might stay around for a few days and just sit on the beach or something like that."

"It would do you good. Is Greg coming out?"

"No."

They choose fruit plates. Her mother asks for ice cream on the side. "I shouldn't, Lizzie, I know I shouldn't."

"Oh, well, once in a while…"

Her mother sips her white wine slowly. "Your dad used to say I would end up like a little butterball. Like my side of the family. He used to joke about that."

"He would."

"Not you, of course, you're tall and skinny like he was…you're like him a lot."

"Actually, I'm starting to spread a bit, too…"

Her mother's fingers with their arthritic knuckles play with the rim of her glass; her eyes are watering at the corners. She talks about old acquaintances, many of whom have died.

When the talking has finished, there is silence. Elizabeth is aware of a sense of strangeness, almost embarrassment.

She waves for the bill to be brought over.

"Can you get home all right?" she asks her mother.

Her mother like Elizabeth has taken the bus downtown—she still can't drive, still refers to the bus as the "streetcar."

She waits with her mother at the bus stop. Her mother has difficulty getting up the steep steps of the bus; Elizabeth rushes over, but the bus driver has taken her arm.

Elizabeth realizes her mother is an old woman.

Why does this come as a revelation?

As does the thought that her father, if he had lived, would be a very old man.

"Goodbye, Mother," she says to her through the open window.

This will be the last dive. They will not visit the deeper stern of the *Anabelle*, and at Elizabeth's insistence she and Karen will not use a buddy line. It is important for Elizabeth to be free for this last visit.

It is very hot. The grass is browning; there has been no rain for a month. This coast shrivels up without water. It suffocates. She is reminded of Toronto in the summer, the nights as hot as the days.

She scans the horizon for some sign of a break in the weather. The sky is a remorseless blue, the colour of Van Gogh's sky, the edges fluted in copper.

She is aware that after this dive, she is interring the wrecks, consigning them to paper. The innocence of the Hausmanns presented as an hypothesis, a mystery which surrounds the last days of Ursula's life.

She would like to see the *White Swan*. To place it in her mind beside the *Anabelle*.

Under the ocean, the plankton bloom fills the air with a Dickensian fog. Thick, murky, it does not sift and break as a land fog might. That is, until they reach the *Anabelle*: the faceplate visibility suddenly clarifies, and the world is illuminated, phosphorescent anemones glittering like lamplight.

She gives Karen the OK sign. It is a good omen, she thinks.

They are among the giant sponges, veering away from the *Anabelle*. They have checked compasses. Elizabeth is hopeful now; in this visibility the *White Swan* might loom into view.

They are tunnelling through the sponges, beside them long ratfish, a wolf eel stares out of a cave in an enormous ledge; the bottom of the ocean alternates between mud and boulders; they reach a meadow of bull kelp, topped by cloud sponges. Carefully they swim around the kelp; there is a sudden clearing. Karen is pointing.

In front of them, in the green clarity, an outline of timbers and ribs of a hull. Karen is nodding vigourously. This is the ship she had found—this is the *White Swan*.

She is badly decomposed, but the stem and the ribs rising from the backbone of the keel are still evident. They have come upon the stern—the wooden rudder protrudes from the mud, its hinges, green and barnacled, still visible. Scattered throughout the mud and rocks are what look like pieces of machinery, possibly pipes, valves.

Elizabeth swims towards the bow. The stern of the *White Swan* ends abruptly in midships—it has been broken in half, the planks are splayed, a gash extends across the width of the ship.

But Tom's work, the heavy oak keel, has remained intact.

Everywhere there is a litter of planks and frames; the cabin has collapsed, as has the *Anabelle*'s, into a pile of debris.

The bow is intact—the wood still joined in a graceful arc, supporting bared ribs.

The water is darkening, a swirl of moving current, changing the clear visibility; with the increasing darkness, the ocean is becoming colder. Karen is by, she is making the "up" sign; Elizabeth shakes her head, gives her a "one minute" sign.

She reaches for her light. She must take another look at the bow.

Something has occurred to her, and the importance of it is overwhelming.

The bow of the *White Swan* is intact.

The bow of the *Anabelle* is smashed into fragments.

Surely, if the *White Swan* had crashed into the *Anabelle*, the *White Swan*'s bow would have been broken up.

Had history been entirely wrong? Jim Rowan had told her he had seen the small ship head for the larger one. Had he told the story often enough that now he believed it?

Had he ever really known what had happened?

It is becoming colder and darker.

Elizabeth feels excitement mounting; she swims around the *White Swan*, mentally checking measurement. Putting together the wounded splinters. Yes, it was right. This boat would be about thirty feet. *The keel—a heavy piece of oak, lying stretched out*—who had told her this? Was it Bess?

The heavy piece of oak had held, Tom's keel is still intact, the *White Swan* fallen into gentler terrain than the *Anabelle* whose after-end dangled over a ledge, and would inevitably topple over.

The *White Swan* is on even terrain.

Elizabeth feels a sense of satisfaction—Ursula's beautiful, expensive ship had no foundation.

All around the *White Swan*, alien mounds—she does not wish to intrude, but her light picks up a jagged edge, and Elizabeth carefully pulls out of the silt a broken tea cup, intact except for its ear. On the bottom of the cup, the words Royal Worcester, England, and Elizabeth is struck by the fact that Bess would have brought good china along for the maiden voyage (and the last) of the *White Swan*. But why not? Did they not dress for dinner in their cabin? She is almost moved to tears; turning the cup in her gloved hands, feeling its surface, stroking it, she debates whether she will bring it to the surface, and then, carefully, puts it back into the silt which has enclosed it for so many years.

Elizabeth can barely contain her excitement; she looks for Karen, her light flashing through the thick darkness. She sees a dim light moving, pocking the black ocean. And then Karen is beside her, giving her the "up" signal, holding herself against the cold, and pointing to her tank. Elizabeth shakes her head. One minute, she signals again. She is going to check the bow, once more, to carve its lines in her memory; she wishes she had brought an underwater camera to photograph what she sees.

Karen is pleading. "UP—danger" she signals, and Elizabeth tells her to go—she will be right behind her...

Karen shakes her head; she starts to inflate her buoyancy jacket and reaches for Elizabeth, but Elizabeth eludes her. She swims quickly towards the stern; she must hurry now—her light picks up the ribs, the crushed planks, the clear formation of the bow. Why did she not bring a camera with her?

She checks her compass; her head feels very strange—she begins to wonder what she is doing there. Why is she staring at a dead ship? It suddenly makes no sense to her. She is having trouble marshalling her thoughts into a straight line—they are broken up, falling all around her. There is no coherence to them. She is freezing cold. Falling. Words run through her head: *First chill, then stupor, then the letting go* —

She wants to let go.

She must get out of this tomb as quickly as possible.

She is rising to the surface through tubes of thick bulbous seaweed which have her still by the throat. And she is sea-sick, shaking violently, swallowing the sea and spewing it up again.

She realizes suddenly that she is not moving, or if she is moving, she is staying in the same place, on a treadmill. Above her, the path out of the ocean, but she cannot reach it. Her body is racked with pain, her legs slowly becoming paralysed, dead weights attached to her torso.

She tries to pray but her words come out in filaments, tiny unrelated specks, paper matter that swims by her and then disappears.

A figure floats towards her. Through the mists she can make out an outline which is at once familiar and yet oddly unremembered.

"Lizzie," a voice says, a voice that reverberates and echoes, till her head is bursting with sound. And yet the voice is out of synch, the words appearing after they have been mouthed, as if the sound were dubbed.

Her father is reaching towards her.

He is very young. Younger, she thinks, than I am. His hair is fine, like the hair of a young child, and waving, pale brown eel grass moving in the water. He is wearing dark heavy oilies, the clothing of the ancient mariners, black, sombre, suitable for Pacific storms.

"Lizzie," he says again. He is close now, his arms are outstretched.

"No," she says. She wonders if he can hear her, her pain is so great.

He stands beside her, his expression eager, expectant.

"I've missed you," he says. The voice, tempered by the hum of the sea, carries old cadences of hurt. "You've missed me, too. I didn't mean to leave you."

"You never left me, Father. Never. I could never erase you."

"I thought so much of you, Lizzie, we were so alike."

"Father..." Now her words are stronger, come out in sharp spurts of indignation. "I had no sense of life apart from you—there was no place to hide—I was caught up in pity..." She is repeating the word over and over, she cannot go on.

"Lizzie," he says, "I am so happy to see you, we are close to Tir nan Og, you and I together..." He smiles at her; the smile is charming, as she knew it would be, radiant, compelling. And empty. She realizes he is not listening to her, has no understanding, is present only to himself.

"I'm not going with you, Father," she says. He moves for her again, he has hold of her hands, she is in his grip, the sea is bubbling around them like a cauldron...

She is going down, swirling, hurtling so quickly she cannot see objects; it is a time tunnel, she is rushing backwards. "You're dead, Father!" She is screaming but the scream has no echo, and pain washes over her in green and yellow patterns, haloed by red. Words are pulled from her throat, "I'm alive," she whispers. Light steadies to pale burning white. Her father has released her. He is stepping back. Into his own time. A sea whip, thick and twisted, sways on the spot.

She stares at the gargoyle. It is too soon for sympathy.

❦

There is a light, but it is dim, the light filtered through swarms of sea bloom, of tiny fish, of waving dark plants.

There are arms which hold her head, cradle her body.

There is a voice, and she is floating on its sounds. And machines that whir like a drowning engine.

She is conscious of a face, familiar and yet not familiar, in waves. She is having a migraine, she thinks, and then she makes out someone in white watching her, there has been darkness, there is a light, faces from the dark, light and dark, Easter vigil, but this face is set, set against a curving ceiling—she is in a tomb…there are two people in white now, a man and a woman, they have come closer. She hears them say she is conscious.

❦

She drifts back into the ocean, and then comes out again. And this time she stays. And they tell her she has been here for several days, and that she has suffered severe decompression sickness, the bends.

She is in Vancouver, in the General Hospital. She thinks, I was born here. Outside and far away the traffic sounds in muted harmony.

She is told her mother has been waiting. Her husband has arrived. "...and the girl who dived with you," the nurse says. Elizabeth knows the girl is carrying flowers, white and green, the colour of sea anemones.

She feels heavy, tired, and as she disappears into sleep, she thinks there is something important she should remember.

It will probably come back to her when she wakes again.